# Kiplinger's

# CAREER STARTER

## Your Game Plan For A
## Successful Job Search

BY JACK O'BRIEN

KIPLINGER BOOKS, Washington, D.C.

**KIPLINGER BOOKS**

Published by
The Kiplinger Washington Editors, Inc.
1729 H Street, N.W.
Washington, D.C. 20006

**Library of Congress Cataloging-in-Publication Data**
O'Brien, Jack, 1936-
    Kiplinger's career starter : your game plan for a successful job search
      by Jack O'Brien.
      p. cm.
      Includes bibliographical references.
      ISBN 0-938721-25-9 : $10.95
        1. Job hunting.  2. Vocational guidance.  I. Title.
HF5382.7.027 1993
650.14—dc20                                                93-3017
                                                        CIP

This publication is intended to provide guidance in regard to the subject matter covered. It is sold with the understanding that the author and publisher are not herein engaged in rendering legal, accounting, tax or other professional services. If such services are required, professional assistance should be sought.

First printing. Printed in the United States of America.

*Book and cover designed by S. Laird Jenkins Corp.*
*Cover illustration by James Mitchell*
*Original drawings by Fred Moore*

*Sources for notes in margins:* the College Placement Council; the National Center for Education Statistics, U.S. Department of Education; *the Monthly Labor Review,* a publication of the U.S. Department of Labor, Bureau of Labor Statistics; *Working Woman* magazine; and the *Current Biography Yearbook.*

# DEDICATION

I dedicate this book to my children—Laura, Pamela, Mark and Megan—who inspired this book; to my parents, Martin and Bernice, who shared work values with all of their children; and my wife, Barbara, who taught me how to balance work with the more important aspects of life. My family continues to be a source of love, inspiration, humor and motivation to share my thoughts with others. Thank you all.

# PREFACE

In 1982 I wrote to my daughter, Laura, telling her how proud I was of her as she approached graduation from Cedar Crest College in Allentown, Pennsylvania. As an afterthought, I added some job hunting tips she could consider as she prepared for the transition from college to the "real world." Laura called me to say everyone had enjoyed a few good laughs over my typical Father-Daughter letter. Then she said that some of her friends had requested a copy of the job hunting advice. I thought it unusual that they had taken my commonsense suggestions so seriously.

In 1986, my son, Mark, prepared to graduate from Elon College in North Carolina. I knew he might need more than a letter, as he had lived college life to the fullest. So, I used my earlier comments to create a planner/organizer notebook for job hunting. To my surprise, Mark actually used the organizer and landed a job within 30 days of graduation. I also found myself reproducing copies of the organizer for Mark's friends. Two more graduations and many improvements later, self-publishing seemed inevitable. It was fun condensing more than 25 years of business experience into a guide that would help someone land a job.

And, now, the organizer has evolved into *Kiplinger's Career Starter*, thanks to my alliance with many people at Kiplinger. This book reflects the commitment of David Harrison, Director of Kiplinger Books, who believed in my concept. I was introduced to David by his assistant Dianne Olsufka, who also proofread the book. This book would not have come to be without the endorsement of Knight Kiplinger, Editor in Chief of *Kiplinger's Personal Finance Magazine* and Co-Editor of *The Kiplinger Washington Letter*. It benefited from the initial interest in my work by Jack Kiesner, Editorial Director of the *Kiplinger Washington Letter*, who was introduced to me by Dick Golden, my friend and retired *Letter* editor.

The final manuscript was the result of diligent work by Amy Ruth, a recent college graduate and my market-research "focus group of one," and Carol Lloyd, my assistant, who has contributed to this project since its inception. My editor, Pat Mertz Esswein, deserves special thanks for encouraging me to "explain it better" and suggesting how to do just that. Fred Moore, a senior at the University of Texas–Arlington, lent his illustrative talents to add a touch of humor. Thanks also to Denise Haney, who smoothed the copy, and to Research Reporter Susan Province, Publicity Director Jennifer Robinson and Production Director Don Fragale.

Jack O'Brien
April 1993

P.S. While working on *Career Starter* a funny thing happened. I realized that my own career should focus on helping young people prepare for their careers. So in 1993, eleven years after writing my letter to Laura, and when many of my colleagues are taking early retirement, I have started a new career. I founded Campus Career Centers, Inc., to privatize college job placement offices. Now we are starting anew together. Best of luck to all of us.

# CONTENTS

# CONTENTS

# INTRODUCTION

**O**ver the years I have talked with many young men and women embarking on their first serious job hunts. They come to me while "networking," and they're looking for specific leads they can follow up. Whether or not I can help them with that, I try to give them something more...my ideas on what makes a first job valuable. I'd like to share these thoughts with you, too, as you set out on this adventure.

What you should seek in your first job isn't the best pay, or job security, or even a clear upward path within that particular company. The best starting jobs are ones in which you'll be:

- worked very hard by managers with high standards,
- taught up-to-date, transferrable skills,
- and given a chance to show your worth.

Your first few jobs should be resumé builders, the kinds of jobs in which you'll learn skills to use for the rest of your life, even if you change jobs or careers several times.

A job like that will be so valuable that the pay should be irrelevant. *You* could pay your *employer* for the privilege of working there, and it would still be a bargain for you. If your first few jobs meet these tests (and you do, too), then your later jobs will come easily.

We at the Kiplinger organization are proud to publish this fine job-search guide by Jack O'Brien. The readers of our periodicals are successful managers, business owners and professional people. They read our *Kiplinger Letters* for judgment on where the economy is headed and how government actions will affect their work. They read *Kiplinger's Personal Finance Magazine* for advice on managing their own money. Our readers are people who understand that, as my grandfather W.M. Kiplinger said, "The times will always be changing. Much of life and work consists of looking for the changes in advance and figuring out what to do about them." That's a practical and proven approach for all times, bad or good.

That's why you should persist in looking for the opportunity you want, regardless of what's said about the economy, the job market, or the outlook for a degree, graduating class, or generation. With the help of your education, your hard work, and a reasonable degree of luck, anything is possible. This book will show you how to put them all together. If you achieve the kind of results you're capable of, we look forward to serving your information needs, too, in a few years.

Best wishes and good luck!

Knight A. Kiplinger
Editor in Chief, *Kiplinger's Personal Finance Magazine*
Co-Editor, *The Kiplinger Washington Letter*

# AN OVERVIEW

Congratulations, you have made an important decision in acquiring *Kiplinger's Career Starter.* Its action-oriented contents will help you be more productive and successful as you launch your career and compete for the job you want.

### What is Career Starter?

*Career Starter* is more than a book. It is a planner/organizer aimed at designing your personal game plan and coaching you through your career development and job campaign.

### Who should use Career Starter?

*Career Starter* is for college students, recent graduates and graduate students, as well as for those whose first or second jobs turned out to be false starts or dead ends.

### Why should you use Career Starter?

The U.S. Department of Labor reports that one of five college graduates in the 1980s had jobs that did not require college degrees. You need *Career Starter* to land a job that provides the rewards you expect from your college investment.

### When should you use Career Starter?

College students could begin to use *Career Starter* after their freshman year. It could help influence choice of major, as well as internships and summer jobs. If you are a college junior, senior or recent graduate, *Career Starter* is just in time to help. Even if you are a college graduate in a low-wage or dead-end position, you can still use *Career Starter* to jump start your career.

# USING CAREER STARTER

*Career Starter* is a no-nonsense, hands-on tool for getting the job you want. To get the most out of it, read *Career Starter* once through completely. This will help you appreciate how helpful the forms and work sheets will be in planning and organizing your job campaign. Then invest in a good three-ring binder, which will eventually become your personal version of *Career Starter*. Go through *Career Starter* again, this time following all the instructions and doing all the exercises in each section. Each section represents one step—or strategy—on the way to getting the job you really want. Those steps are:

1. **Why Will You Work?** Part One helps you identify your work values, interests and skills. The exercises will help you determine what kind of career matches your strengths, needs and future goals.

2. **Preparing for Today's Work World.** Part Two shows you where to find today's jobs. Evaluate the prospects for your career based on the information you find in Part Two.

3. **Planning Your Job Campaign.** Part Three provides forms and work sheets that lead you through the job campaign process and offers tips on surviving financially during your job search.

4. **Organizing Your Job Campaign.** Part Four helps you arrange your job campaign activities into manageable tasks. It also teaches you where to find valuable information that can help you make intelligent career decisions.

5. **When You're Marketing Yourself.** Part Five shows you how to present, promote, position and price yourself in today's job market.

*First Job: Bob Kerrey, senator from Nebraska and presidential hopeful in 1992, opened Grandmother's Skillet restaurant with his brother-in-law in Omaha.*

3

## Job Offers By Major

*The percentage of job offers, by area of study, made to 1992 graduates:*

| | |
|---|---|
| **Business** | **39.2%** |
| **Engineering** | **35.4%** |
| **Humanities and** | |
| **Social Sciences** | **6.4%** |
| **Computer Sciences** | **5.5%** |
| **Health Sciences** | **3.1%** |
| **Education** | **3.0%** |
| **Communications** | **2.9%** |
| **Sciences** | |
| **(inc. Math)** | **2.5%** |
| **Home Economics** | **1.0%** |
| **Agriculture & Natural** | |
| **Resources** | **1.0%** |

6. **Job Campaign Tactics That Work.** Part Six offers suggestions for competing for the job you want. You can also learn how to outwit and outmaneuver your job competitors.

7. **Interviewing for First Place.** In Part Seven, you learn the art of persuading your prospective employer that you are the best qualified candidate for the job.

8. **Time to Make a Decision.** Part Eight shows you how to gracefully accept or decline a job offer. By working through the "Job Offer Evaluation" work sheet, you can decide whether this job is the one for you. It also offers advice for success in your new career.

## *Four Important Points Before You Begin*

1. **Research will be a big part of your job campaign strategy**—the more you know, the better able you will be to compete for the job you want. Throughout *Career Starter,* you will find discussion of how to research your options, career fields, companies or prospective employers. For example, in Part Four, "Organizing Your Job Campaign," you will be introduced to resources such as the public library, trade and professional organizations, and electronic information services. Remember to use all your resources to their fullest potential.

2. **The key to converting *Career Starter* to your personal game plan is to write things down.** By putting your thoughts in writing, you transform theory into reality. You make probable what was previously only possible. In addition, you start a process that makes things happen. Then, you'll have something to react to. The result is a game plan that will work for you.

**3. Your** *Career Starter* **will help with your record keeping** by providing the following work sheets as well as suggestions on how to use them for best results. Look for the "copy" insignia that identifies each one.

- Work Value Assessment (page 9)
- Personal Interests (page 11)
- Skills Inventory (page 12-13)
- Job Campaign Plan (page 30)
- Monthly Cash Flow (page 35)
- Daily Job Campaign Calendar (page 39)
- Networking Directory (page 55)
- Resumé Checklist (page 63)
- Action Log (page 73)
- Job Prospect Profile (page 90-91)
- Job Campaign Improvement Suggestions (page 119)
- Job Offer Evaluation (page 123)

**4. Create your personal** *Career Starter* **notebook** by reproducing all of the forms and placing them in a three-ring binder with tabs. This makes it convenient to add information as you progress in your job campaign and easier to locate the information you need when you need it. Remember, if you do the right things right, you will be successful in your job campaign.

PART

ONE

# WHY WILL YOU WORK?

## Assessing Your Work Values

**W**ork is a key element of our existence, in every phase of our development. We work to realize our dreams, develop our potential, and obtain the material goods we need to survive and prosper. Work lets us contribute productively to our families, communities and our world. Through work, we can fulfill a mission.

To make proper career choices, you must place the acquisition of material and nonmaterial wealth in proper balance from your own perspective. You might call this balancing your checkbook with your values. The question you have to answer is "What do I want to be?" rather than, "What do I want to have?" When you know what motivates you, you can then begin to make career decisions with more satisfying results. Use the following list of work values and related careers to help you think about and assess your work values. This list isn't intended to be all inclusive. However, it will help you get started. This is the beginning of a lifelong process. Every job you take on will help you refine or expand your thinking. Good luck!

## Work Values and Related Careers

| Work Value | Related Career |
|---|---|
| Care for the Earth | Conservation, Non-Profit Activism, Politics, Agriculture, Geology, Marine Biology, Forestry Service |
| Help Others | Health Services, Social Services, Special Education, Nursing Home Administration, Missionary Service, Peace Corps |
| Improve Society | Non-Profit Foundations, Education, Religion, Law Enforcement, Medicine |
| Share Knowledge | Education, Writing, Research, Religion |
| Create | Design, Any Job! |
| Meet Others | Sales, Tourism, Politics, Hotel/Restaurant Management, Promotion |
| Feed the World | Agriculture, Animal Husbandry, Private Volunteer Organizations |
| Build | Construction, Architecture, Sculpting, Catering |
| Gain Fame | Television, Radio, Theater, Politics, Philanthropy |
| Gain Experience | Any Job! |
| Use New Technology | Computer Systems Management, Science, Industry, Space Exploration, Invention, Medicine |
| Travel | International Business, Airlines, Wholesale Business, Importing/Exporting, Travel Arranging, Politics, Missionary Work, Diplomatic Service |
| Be Physically Active | Health & Fitness Instruction/Administration, Professional Sports, Natural Resources Management, Any Work Outdoors |
| Direct/Lead Others | Military Service, Education, Management |
| Serve the Public | Government, Law Enforcement, Education, Social Services |
| Work Independently | Free-lance Writing, Research, Free-lance Photography, Consulting of Any Kind, the Arts |
| Stimulate my Intellect | Research of Any Kind, Library Administration, University Education and Administration, Publishing |
| Work at Home | Anything Using Computers, Day Care, Crafts/Sewing |
| Achieve Financial Security | Own Your Own Business |
| Make Money | All of the Above |
| Accomplish Much With Pride | Any Job! |
| Achieve Self-Fulfillment | See the Following |

## Work Value Assessment

Now start thinking about your work values. Fill in the spaces below with the top five to ten work values you believe are most important to you, including any that weren't on our list of examples, and describe why they're important to you. You may wish to discuss this exercise with someone who knows you well and can give you objective input, such as a roommate, professor or close friend.

*Important Work Values*                    *Why They're Important to Me*

1. _____    _____

2. _____    _____

3. _____    _____

4. _____    _____

5. _____    _____

6. _____    _____

7. _____    _____

8. _____    _____

9. _____    _____

10. _____    _____

Don't worry, there are no "correct" answers. This exercise is simply meant to help you know yourself better. Chances are the results don't surprise you, but now you have a valuable profile of yourself on paper that you can refer to again. Compare this list with your interest list, which follows.

## Identifying Your Interests

Successful people don't realize they're working because they are having too much fun. They sometimes exceed their own potential because they are so passionate about what they are doing. So, if you want to be happy in your work, find something that is important to your well-being and that you can do passionately. Combining what you love with what you need is an important key to success. The following sample links passions to careers possibilities.

| Passion | Career |
| --- | --- |
| Art | Cultural Activities, Museum Administration, Education, Gallery Management, Fine Arts |
| Sports | Leisure Events, Professional Athletics, Coaching/Training |
| Travel | Writing, Photography, Tour Operation |
| The Elderly | Health Care, Nursing Home Administration |
| Outdoors | Construction, Botany, Forestry Service, Park Service |
| Travel Overseas | Peace Corps, Importing/Exporting, Military Service |
| Physical Activity | Coaching, Training, Aerobics/Dance Instruction, Agriculture |
| Problem-Solving | Customer Service, Politics, Science, Management, Medicine, Any Job! |
| Money | Commissioned Sales, Banking, Investing |
| Technology | Telecommunications, Industry, Science |
| Food | Cooking, Catering, Food Service, Restaurant Management, Food Writing |
| Reading | Library Science, Editorial Services, Education, Research, Publishing |
| Music | Entertainment, Radio Production/Management, Artist Promotion/Management |
| Clothes | Retailing, Fashion Design, Fashion Merchandising, Sewing/Tailoring |
| Children | Day Care, Elementary Education |
| The Environment | Air, Water or Waste Management, Non-Profit Activism, Natural Resources/Wildlife Management, Manufacturing Process Management |
| Crafts | Interior Design, Graphic Design, Clothing or Home Furnishings Design and Construction |
| People With Disabilities | Physical Therapy, Social Work, Special Education |
| Creativity | Desktop Publishing, Advertising, Marketing, Catering, Architecture |
| Games | Computer Systems, Product Testing, Retailing |

## Personal Interests

Based on the results of the preceding exercise, go back and rank your top five to ten personal interests by priority.

1. _____

2. _____

3. _____

4. _____

5. _____

6. _____

7. _____

8. _____

9. _____

10. _____

## Taking Inventory of Your Career-Related Skills

To make a successful career choice, you must match your interests with your skills.

Career-counseling services at local universities and community colleges often offer career testing: interest, aptitude and personality tests. *Interest tests* translate your likes and dislikes into relevant vocational options. *Aptitude tests* reveal your ability to do certain types of work well. *Personality tests* provide information about characteristics that make you suitable for a particular occupation. While these tests do not add up to one prescribed course of action, they are usually very helpful in determining your strengths, weaknesses, likes and dislikes, and in evaluating career options. They are also an objective way to confirm your own hunches, and the value of the information generally exceeds the reasonable costs.

In the meantime, use the quick self-assessment below to get you started. Identify your relevant skills in each category, citing a specific example. These skills are not job-specific. As with all the lists in this book, this list is a starting point. You can expand it or limit it as you choose.

| Category | Career-Related Skill | Your Specific Skill |
|---|---|---|
| **Communication** | Write Well | _____ |
| | Speak Well | _____ |
| | Speak a Foreign Language Fluently | _____ |
| **Critical Thinking** | Identify Issues | _____ |
| | Analyze Options | _____ |
| | Create Solutions | _____ |
| **Computer Literacy** | Know Word Processing Programs | _____ |
| | Know Spreadsheet Programs | _____ |
| | Know Graphics Programs | _____ |
| **Leadership** | Set the Example | _____ |
| | Coach Others | _____ |
| | Guide a Group | _____ |
| **Management** | Set Goals | _____ |
| | Establish Priorities | _____ |
| | Manage Time/Money | _____ |
| **Human Relations** | Be a Team Player | _____ |
| | Fulfill Commitments | _____ |
| | Respect Other Opinions | _____ |
| **Interpersonal** | Follow Instruction | _____ |
| | Build Skills | _____ |
| | Use Common Sense | _____ |

## Career-Related Skills Inventory and Development

### *Career-Related Skills Inventory*

Using the results of the preceding exercise as a basis, now rank your top five to ten skills in order of your personal proficiency.

1. _____
2. _____
3. _____
4. _____
5. _____
6. _____
7. _____
8. _____
9. _____
10. _____

### *Skills Development*

Now, write down the skills, in order of preference, that you would most like to develop.

1. _____
2. _____
3. _____
4. _____
5. _____
6. _____
7. _____
8. _____
9. _____
10. _____

# DECIDING WHAT YOU WANT TO DO

**H**aving assessed your work values, identified your interests and inventoried your skills, you should now have a good idea of what you do or do not want to be. Once you know what you want to be, deciding what you want to do is easy. However, all of us do not get to this milestone prior to our first attempt at a career. Some of us have to experience a career first, then make changes based upon what we have learned. This trial and error method is a valid approach because we learn from experience. However, we want to avoid obvious career mismatches as much as possible. The following five suitability questions may help prevent you from starting off in the wrong direction.

## *Five Career Suitability Questions*

1. Would I stay in this career if I didn't get paid for a period of time?
   *This "love versus money" question may be the real litmus test of what you want to do.*

2. Do I want to spend the next seven to ten years working in this career?
   *This will be the average length of a career in the early twenty-first century.*

3. Am I comfortable with the people in this field?
   *If you can't relate to the people involved, you probably don't belong here.*

4. What is the future for this career?
   *There are few opportunities in a dead-end career.*

5. What can I contribute over time?
   *Visualize your role and responsibilities in this field three to five years from now.*

---

**Most Popular Majors Among Males by Race**

**White**

| | |
|---|---|
| Business and Management | 28% |
| Social Sciences | 14% |
| Engineering | 10% |

**Black**

| | |
|---|---|
| Business and Management | 27% |
| Social Sciences | 13% |
| Engineering | 6% |

**Hispanic**

| | |
|---|---|
| Business and Management | 24% |
| Social Sciences | 13% |
| Engineering | 11% |

**Asian/Pacific Island**

| | |
|---|---|
| Engineering | 25% |
| Business and Management | 19% |
| Social Sciences | 11% |

**American Indian/ Alaskan Native**

| | |
|---|---|
| Business and Management | 21% |
| Social Sciences | 14% |
| Education | 9% |

You will have to find your own answers to these questions. There are no approved solutions. However, just thinking about these issues should provide a clearer focus of what might be best for you.

Use some of the following publications to research your options and find out about available and appropriate careers. You may also want to interview experts in various career fields prior to reaching any firm conclusions. (For more about information interviews, see Part Four, page 53.)

## Suggested Reading

- *What Color Is Your Parachute?*
  Richard Nelson Bolles, Ten Speed Press

- *Careering and Re-Careering for the 1990s:*
  *Skills and Strategies for Shaping Your Future*
  Ronald L. Krannich, Impact Publications

- *Soar If You Dare*
  James R. Ball, Humdinger Books

## Suggested Career Software

If you have access to an IBM-compatible personal computer, the following software can be very helpful. Both programs act as automated mentors for self-directed career- and job-search assistance.

- *Career Design*
  Career Design Software, Atlanta
  (404) 321-6100

- *Career Navigator*
  Drake Beam Morin, Inc., New York
  (212) 692-7700

**Most Popular Majors Among Females by Race**

**White**
| Business and Management | 20% |
| Education | 16% |
| Health Sciences | 9% |

**Black**
| Business and Management | 25% |
| Social Sciences | 11% |
| Health Sciences | 10% |

**Hispanic**
| Business and Management | 20% |
| Education | 12% |
| Social Sciences | 11% |

**Asian/Pacific Island**
| Business and Management | 24% |
| Social Sciences | 11% |
| Life Sciences | 9% |

**American Indian/Alaskan Native**
| Education | 18% |
| Business and Management | 17% |
| Social Sciences | 10% |

# QUALITY OF LIFE IN THE '90S

**W**hile money is a critical factor in your job/career decisions, the opportunity for personal growth and how you spend your free time are equally important. No amount of money can make up for having the wrong job in the wrong place at the wrong time. Here are five guidelines for evaluating the quality of life as it relates to your career.

*Tracy Chapman, singer and songwriter, earned her bachelor's degree in cultural anthropology at Tufts University.*

*Joan Rivers, comedienne and talk show host, earned her bachelor's in English and anthropology at Barnard College in New York City.*

- **Experience**
  There is no substitute for experience. Sometimes it is necessary to accept a low-level job in your field of choice in order to gain entry and acquire valuable experience.

- **Lifetime Learning**
  Education and personal growth are more closely related than most people realize. To make yourself more marketable, you need to build your skills every day. Company-sponsored training programs as well as company-paid educational opportunities are critical for career advancement. To make yourself and your life more interesting, take classes for fun—not grades.

- **Recreation**
  Opportunities for leisure activities are important to prevent personal doldrums, dullness and burn-out. We all need to refresh our minds and bodies for the daily challenges of the workplace.

- **Location**
  Many of today's jobs are location-independent and you may have more choices of where to locate. Don't rule out smaller or medium-size cities; many offer a quality cultural scene without big city prices or hassles.

• **Affordable Living**

If all of your money goes toward housing and commuting, you won't have much left for the fun things. Be able to live within your means.

Considering these work-related issues will help you lead a happier and more productive life, regardless of your career choice.

By now you should know more about yourself and the direction you want to take with your career. The information you have gained will be helpful in writing your resumé, networking and interviewing. Each of those activities is an important element of the job campaign process, and each is discussed in detail in your *Career Starter.*

**PART**

**TWO**

# PREPARING FOR TODAY'S WORK WORLD

# FROM SCHOOL TO THE REAL WORLD

Schoolbook learning and career success are not necessarily related. In school, you learn to learn. At work, you apply learning to a purpose. School learning is an individual effort. In the work environment, teamwork is essential. In school, tools such as computers are usually banned during examinations. At work, one can hardly survive without a computer. In many school settings, you read and listen to lectures. In the world of work, you learn from experience. To make the transition from school to work, consider taking courses in the following subjects either while you are still in school or after you graduate.

- **Business communications,** to learn how to write and speak in the business world.

- **Computer literacy,** to learn how to use at least one word processing, one spreadsheet and one database or desktop publishing application.

- **Interpersonal skills,** to help you work more easily and effectively with others.

- **New career tools,** to equip you with, for example, a foreign language or accounting skills.

- **Your passion,** to make you even more knowledgeable about it.

*Charles Robb, senator from Virginia, earned a bachelor's degree in business administration at the University of Wisconsin.*

*Perry Ellis, fashion designer, deceased, earned a bachelor's degree in business at the College of William and Mary in Williamsburg, Va.*

## *A Word for Liberal Arts Majors*

If you are a liberal arts major questioning the value of your degree in today's work world, relax. You are well-educated. Now you need to transfer your personal skills into the workplace and develop new job-specific skills. If you want to become a manager, you must be willing to develop basic skills first—learn from the ground up. Look for paralegal, research assis-

## Translating Your Major to a Career

If you have made a decision regarding your college major prior to thinking about your chosen career, the following list may help link your college major to a career. Compare your major to your work values, interests and skills identified in Part One, "Why Will You Work?". Look for a consistent pattern or tendency that will point you toward the right career for you.

| College Major | Career Field | College Major | Career Field |
|---|---|---|---|
| Art | Decorating/Design<br>Computer Graphics<br>Media Production<br>Gallery Management<br>Architecture | English | Paralegal Services<br>Technical Writing<br>Journalism<br>Desktop Publishing<br>Information Systems<br>  Management<br>Library Management<br>Law<br>Teaching<br>Publishing<br>Mediation/Arbitration<br>Church Work |
| Business | Administration/<br>  Management<br>Accounting/Finance<br>Marketing/Sales<br>Manufacturing<br>International Trade | | |
| Communications | Advertising<br>Market Research<br>Media Management<br>Public Relations<br>Publishing<br>Mediation/Arbitration | Health Sciences | Insurance<br>Medical Administration<br>Physical Therapy<br>Radiologic Technology<br>Public Health Agencies<br>Teaching |
| Economics | Financial Services<br>Government<br>  Research/Service<br>Trade Associations<br>The Non-Profit Sector | Journalism | Market Research<br>Advertising<br>Books, Newspapers,<br>  Magazines<br>Trade Associations<br>Publishing |

tant or administrative assistant jobs, where your reading, analytical and writing abilities can be utilized. Become computer literate. Ideally, find an employer that offers a training program or a mentor who can teach you the workplace skills you need. If you are a people person, look for work in sales or customer service. Above all, view your liberal arts education as an advantage—because it gives you a strong base upon which to build.

| College Major | Career Field | College Major | Career Field |
|---|---|---|---|
| **Journalism, (cont'd.)** | Information System Management<br>Library Management<br>Law<br>Teaching<br>Mediation/Arbitration | **Political Science and Government** | Government Service<br>Diplomatic Service<br>Politics<br>Law<br>Trade Associations<br>Transportation<br>Land Use Planning |
| **Languages** | Publishing<br>Customer Service<br>Tour Operations<br>Human/Social Services<br>Telecommunications<br>Importing/Exporting<br>Diplomatic Service<br>Law Enforcement<br>Peace Corps<br>Church or Missionary Work | **Psychology** | Advertising<br>Clinical Research and Services<br>Public Relations<br>Sales<br>Market Research |
| **Music** | Entertainment<br>Instrument Sales<br>Publishing<br>Teaching<br>Church Work | **Recreation** | Hospitality Services<br>Resort Management<br>Travel and Tourism<br>Theme Park Activities<br>City/County Programs<br>Event Planning |
| **Mathematics/ Sciences** | Computer Programming/ Software Design<br>Systems Analysis<br>Environmental Services<br>Teaching<br>Research and Development<br>Engineering<br>Manufacturing<br>Military Service<br>Architecture | **Social Sciences** | Paralegal Services<br>Government Service<br>The Non-Profit Sector<br>Philanthropic Foundations<br>Market Research/ Planning<br>Advertising/ Public Relations |

# SHIFTING WITH CORPORATE AMERICA

**M**ost new jobs will come from smaller-growing companies with fewer than 500 employees, not large, restructuring companies. And, many of the new jobs will be in mid-size areas (cities with less than 500,000 population) rather than in major urban centers.

To identify growing companies, follow this three-step procedure:

1. Choose the type of employer and/or geographic location you desire.

2. Based on this criteria, search the resources listed below to target organizations of interest to you.

3. Call or write each targeted firm's public relations, marketing or public information office to obtain an annual report, product and/or service information, organization charts, and the names and titles of key people to contact.

An annual report will tell you if the firm is growing and profitable. It typically provides a history of growth, successes, new products and/or services and financial status. Many times it includes an outlook for the next year. Some privately owned companies probably won't publish an annual report, so ask for a press kit instead.

## *Information Sources*

There are numerous sources of information about organizations. They include the following:

- **Directories**
  Geographic, business, occupational, professional, industry and financial directories are available in your public library. These directories provide information about an organization's products and/or services, number of employees, principal executives, annual revenues, and location(s). (See also Part Four, "Organizing Your Job Campaign.")

- **Trade Associations**
  These organizations produce membership directories, journals and newsletters. They also hold conferences that may serve your networking purposes. Remember, almost every field or industry is affiliated with a trade association. (See Part Four, page 45.)

- **Newspapers**
  The business section of most newspapers contains numerous articles about local companies and their activities. Look for new-product announcements, executive promotions (for key names) and notices of corporate expansions. Also, keep up with news, trends and government activity, and scan the society pages for potential contacts.

- **Electronic Information Services**
  Computer resources for researching companies are available via your personal computer or many college- and career-reference libraries. You can select any field or company and within seconds find what you want to know. A warning: You have to know how to access the information, and the cost can be excessive. (See Part Four, pages 43-44.)

*In 1992, prospective employers offered the highest average salary—$41,567—to undergrads earning bachelor's degrees in pharmacy.*

# WHERE THE JOBS ARE EMERGING

**No** matter how qualified you are, a job opening must exist to make a match. Metropolitan areas in the U.S. that lead in job opportunities are published annually in various periodicals. As with job growth in smaller companies, the most rapid geographical job growth is in areas with less than 500,000 in population. In other words, there is a downsizing in location as well as corporate structure. With this in mind, consider these five location criteria:

1. Smaller growing companies are locating in states with business-friendly environments, such as Washington, Oregon, the Carolinas, Utah and Tennessee.

2. University towns offer opportunity for those who like the college connection. States such as Nebraska, Indiana, Virginia and the Carolinas have universities that are acting as incubators, which provide start-up space, advice and support for new businesses.

3. Growing retirement areas—such as Florida, Arizona, Arkansas, Nevada, New Mexico and Texas—provide great opportunities in agencies and businesses providing services to the elderly.

4. Resort areas, such as Colorado, Tennessee, Florida and Texas, offer jobs as well as fun.

5. Check out the sleepers. Those include states such as Idaho, Iowa, Missouri, and the Dakotas where businesses are growing because of the lower cost of living and of doing business.

## Suggested Reading

- *The New Corporate Frontier: The Move to Small Town USA*
  D.A. Heenan, McGraw Hill

## 24 Cities Experiencing Job Growth

For detailed information regarding any of these areas, write the local Chamber of Commerce in each city.

Albuquerque, NM
Austin, TX
Bloomington, IN
Boise, ID
Charleston, SC
Charlotte, NC
Charlottesville, VA
Columbus, OH
Des Moines, IA
Eugene, OR
Fort Myers—Cape Coral, FL
Greenville—Spartansburg, SC
Knoxville, TN
Las Vegas, NV
Lexington, KY
Lincoln, NE
Nashville, TN
Portland, OR
Raleigh-Durham, NC
Salt Lake City, UT
Scranton—Wilkes-Barre, PA
Spokane, WA
Springfield, MO
Wilmington, NC

# THE INTERNATIONAL SCENE

Today's economic headlines signaling a "global economy" have created visions of working-vacation opportunities. The reality is that there is no such thing as a global job market. So before you start to conduct a global job search, consider the following:

- Local nationals tend to get hired before foreigners.

- It is less expensive for a company to hire locally.

- To compete against local nationals, you must have a unique skill they don't have.

- Even if you have the technical expertise, language skills and legal approvals, you may not have the knowledge and sensitivity to establish effective working relationships in a culture you didn't grow up in.

If your romantic visions are now more tempered and you are still interested in the international field, what should you do? Your best bet is to work in the U.S. for a firm operating overseas. Get to know the basics and develop the necessary skills and then you can move on. Think globally but look locally.

## *Suggested Reading*

If you are determined to work overseas now, here are some resources you may wish to use in your campaign:

- *The Directory of Jobs and Careers Abroad*
  Alex Lipinski, Peterson's, Princeton, NJ

- *Passport to Overseas Employment*
  Dale Chambers, Simon & Schuster

- *Directory of Overseas Summer Jobs*
  edited by David Woodworth, Peterson's

- *The Peace Corps and More:*
  *114 Ways To Work, Study and Travel the World*
  Medea Benjamin, Global Exchange, San Francisco

*In 1992, prospective employers offered the lowest average salary—$17,371—to students earning bachelor's degrees in pre-elementary education.*

**PART**

**THREE**

# PLANNING YOUR JOB CAMPAIGN

# TURNING WISHES INTO ACTION

**B**y now you should be aware of your career values, interests and skills. Also, you should be able to link these issues to the current workplace. The next step is to plan your personal job campaign. The major elements of any job campaign are:

- Establishing your career goals.

- Planning your job campaign.

- Organizing your job campaign.

- Preparing marketing materials.

- Carrying out job campaign tactics.

- Obtaining feedback, evaluating results and making adjustments.

All of the elements are discussed in your *Career Starter*. Once you're familiar with them, you'll be ready to prepare your job campaign plan.

A plan will make your job search easier, less frustrating and more successful. Visualize what you want to be, then translate that vision into a job campaign goal. Determine a strategy to reach your goal. Next, list the major steps necessary to implement that strategy. Finally, target and contact the key people who can help you. (See the sample Job Campaign Plan on page 29.)

Remember, everyone works with a different timetable. The trick is to find what works for you and stick with it. If you can afford to take the summer off after graduation, relax and enjoy yourself—you will probably spend the rest of your life working. If you don't have that luxury, you'll want to begin your job campaign well before graduation.

*Dick Clark, TV personality and producer, earned his bachelor's degree in advertising from Syracuse University.*

*Kevin Costner, actor, film producer and director, earned a bachelor's degree in marketing at California State University at Fullerton.*

# HOW TO USE YOUR JOB CAMPAIGN PLAN

*Garry Shandling, comedian and TV personality, earned his bachelor's in marketing from the University of Arizona.*

**U**se your Job Campaign Plan to get started in the right direction and to keep moving ahead on target. Your plan contains your job goal, your job campaign strategy to achieve that goal, key steps to carry out your strategy, and the names of people you need to contact to make things happen. Because planning is a process, your plan should be updated weekly. The elements of your plan are:

- **Job Goal**
  State what you want to be with what type of organization and what skills you bring to the job. This same goal may be stated in your resumé. (See Part Five, page 58.)

- **Job Search Strategy**
  What is your overall approach to achieve your goal? What resources will you utilize? (See Part Four, page 40.)

- **Major Tasks to Carry Out Strategy**
  What are the important tasks you need to perform to carry out your job campaign strategy? (See Parts Four, Five and Six.)

- **Key People to Contact**
  Nothing happens until you start talking with people. Who are the people you need to talk with to develop your network of contacts? (See Part Four, page 49.)

- **Comments**
  Write down any details you may want to refer to later that have not been listed above.

You should not finalize your job campaign plan until you are familiar with all the parts of your *Career Starter.* However, it is never too early to start thinking about the critical elements of your plan and to make notes for future reference. Review the following sample Job Campaign Plan.

## Sample Job Campaign Plan

### Job Goal

_Obtain a position as a writer with a public relations firm utilizing my degree in English, my word_ _processing and desktop publishing skills, and my staff writing experience._

### Job Search Strategy

_Develop a network of contacts using the Public Relations Society of America (PRSA) and members_ _of my personal network._

### Major Tasks to Carry Out Strategy

1. _Contact PRSA to obtain Washington, DC, membership list and information packet_
2. _Write resumé and cover letter_
3. _Target individuals for information interviews_
4. _Script telephone approach_
5. _Prepare list of questions for information interview_

### Key People to Contact

1. _Director of Communications—Public Relations Society of America_
2. _Friend who works for Greater Washington Society for Association Executives_
3. _Friend who is staff aide for U.S. Congressman_
4. _Friend at travel agency who uses public relations firm_
5. _Brother's friend who is building manager with public relations firm tenant_
6. _College business communications instructor_
7. _Friend of friend who works as reporter for the Washington Post_
8. _Friend of parents who is manager of an advertising firm_
9. _Friend of friend who works for personnel search firm_
10. _Friend of friend who works for government contractor doing environmental clean-up_

### Comments

_Organize work space_

_Read ads in Sunday newspapers_

_Notify friends regarding job campaign_

# Job Campaign Plan

*Job Goal*

_____

_____

*Job Search Strategy*

_____

_____

*Major Tasks to Carry Out Strategy*

1. _____
2. _____
3. _____
4. _____
5. _____

*Key People to Contact*

1. _____
2. _____
3. _____
4. _____
5. _____
6. _____
7. _____
8. _____
9. _____
10. _____

*Comments*

# SURVIVING WHILE YOU CAMPAIGN

Too bad academe never offered courses on cash flow, expense budgeting or credit management. The economic realities of living on your own, especially while you're trying to launch your career, can be overwhelming. Food, rent, clothing, transportation and school loans all seem to hit at once. Then your parents explain that you now have to obtain your own health insurance, car insurance and phone credit card. The lure of instant money via credit cards is a trap awaiting many unsuspecting big spenders. Numerous small purchases add up faster than you realize. All these expenses and no income. It doesn't seem fair. What do you do? Here are some tips:

## *Shelter*

- If you are job-searching near your parents' home, ask to live with them during your search. Establish a written agreement with your parents regarding monthly payments, terms and conditions, such as duration, as well as rights and responsibilities of both parties. This helps establish a mutual understanding that can make life easier for everyone.

- Because you may lack steady income, you may wish to establish a barter system with your parents. For example, in exchange for room and board, you can wash cars, cut grass, pick up groceries, cook some meals and take out the trash.

*The six most popular majors at four-year colleges in 1992 were, in this order: business administration and management, education, psychology, accounting, engineering and computer science.*

- Accept the fact that although you have been semi-independent for the last few years, it is difficult for your parents to stop trying to take care of you after twenty-plus years, especially while you are living at home. Also, try to do chores that need to be done without having to be asked.

- If family or friends do not have room for you, check the classified ads for house-sitting opportunities or for room rentals in private homes.

- If you are job-searching away from home, try to find temporary shelter with people who travel much of the time, such as auditors, flight attendants, or people who work different shifts, such as nurses or law enforcement officers. Establish an agreement to pay a portion of the rent week to week or month to month. Do not sign a lease unless it is month-to-month only.

## Health Insurance

- Coverage under your parents' policy usually ends when you stop being a full-time student or when you reach age 23 or 25, depending on the policy. Once you have a job, you may be able to join the employer-sponsored group coverage.

- Insurers offer short-term (three, six or twelve months) policies at reasonable cost. Such policies may be renewable, typically for up to a year. Also, any major illness during this time may be excluded from coverage on a future policy due to a common clause concerning pre-existing conditions.

## Transportation

- Don't buy a car until you have a job. Even then, wait until you have your expenses under control. Ask about discounts for recent college graduates.

- Remember, a car means extra costs for insurance, taxes and maintenance.

- A nearly new car (less than a year old) can cost thousands less than a new car.

- Many larger cities have companies that rent used cars for a short while, like a week or month.

- Walk, ride your bike or use public transportation when possible.

## Credit Cards

- Limit yourself to one general-purpose credit card that has no annual fee.

- Maintain a balance of less than $500 or 50% of what you have in a savings account. Make your monthly payments on time.

- Special-purpose credit cards, such as telephone and gasoline cards, are for convenience—not borrowing. Pay them in full each month.

## Clothing

- Maintain a basic interview wardrobe that's always clean and pressed.

- Don't buy any clothing that is not discounted at least 20%.

## Money

- Once you have a job, develop a monthly budget—including savings—and stick to it.

- Maintain at least $1,000 in your savings account for emergencies.

*In 1992, students receiving the most job offers were those who earned bachelor's degrees in accounting, mechanical engineering and electrical engineering.*

- Remember you are starting to establish a credit history that is important to your career. Many companies conduct credit checks as part of a complete background investigation prior to issuing a job offer.

## *Taxes*

- Chances are you'll be starting a job mid-year or later, so you will be using the standard deduction when filing your taxes. Regardless, job search expenses for your first job are not deductible. After that, expenses must exceed 2% of your adjusted gross income, and you must be searching for a job in the same line of work.

- If you expect to work continuously for no more than about eight months during the year, ask your employer to use a special part-year method to compute your withholding for taxes. This method is based on actual earnings, versus a full year's earnings, and will provide more take-home pay.

## Monthly Cash Flow Work Sheet

If you haven't already begun to track your income and expenses, it's a great habit to develop, even if you aren't currently receiving a regular paycheck.

Reproduce one copy of the work sheet for each month of the year. That will allow you to account for items that may change from month to month. File your work sheets in a separate section at the back of your personal *Career Starter* notebook.

If you need to cut back, focus first on expenses unrelated to survival and a successful job search. Remember, living cheaply can mean greater independence and adventure. It could even become a way of life.

**Month** _____

### Income

Wages, salary, tips
  (after taxes)    $ _____

Loans _____

Gifts _____

**Total Income**    $ _____


### Expenses

Job Search (inc. supplies/
  printing, postage,
  long-distance telephone,
  special travel) _____

Rent (or mortgage) _____

Food (groceries) _____

Utilities (inc. electricity,
  gas, oil, water/sewer,
  garbage, telephone) _____

Savings (for emergencies,
  investments, vacations,
  other) _____

Public Transportation
  (inc. parking) _____

Auto Loan _____

Auto Insurance _____

Misc. Auto Expenses (gas, oil,
  repairs, fees and taxes) _____

Health Insurance _____

Medical, Dental and
  Eye-Care Bills Not
  Covered by Insurance _____

Credit Card Payments _____

Loan Payments _____

Clothing (inc. dry
  cleaning, laundry) _____

Personal Care (inc. hair cuts) _____

Home Maintenance
  (inc. furnishings, paint) _____

Educational Expenses _____

Recreation/Entertainment
  (inc. eating out, movies,
  clubs, cable TV, CDs,
  books, gym membership) _____

Vacations _____

Gifts _____

**Total Expenses**    $ _____

**Total Income**    $ _____

**Total Expenses**    – _____

**Total Cash Flow,**
**or Discretionary Income**    $ _____

P A R T

F O U R

# ORGANIZING YOUR JOB CAMPAIGN

## GETTING IT TOGETHER

*Career Starter* will help you get organized by teaching you to arrange your job campaign activities into manageable tasks and schedule activities in the right order for maximum productivity. You'll also want to:

- Keep all critical information regarding your job campaign in your *Career Starter* notebook for convenience and effective follow-up.

- Select a specific location in your home dedicated to your job campaign activities. Ideally, it should contain a desk or table, chair, lamp, telephone, filing box with folders and large wastebasket.

- Buy an answering machine to receive return calls while you are out.

- If you have a personal computer, organize your campaign activities separate from other applications. This way, you can access your files quickly during a telephone call.

- Choose a calendar—a very personal decision. Monthly calendars provide the long-term picture. Weekly calendars provide a more manageable timetable and daily calendars provide a specific schedule of tasks to be accomplished that day.

Remember, when you're organized, good things happen. It's that simple.

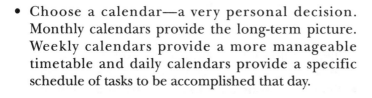

# HOW TO USE YOUR DAILY JOB CAMPAIGN CALENDAR

*More people were enrolled in law school in 1989 than were awarded law degrees between 1955 and 1972.*

The key to success is to use the type of calendar with which you are most comfortable. Usually a combination works best for most of us in most situations. However, in a job campaign, you need a calendar that produces results. The Daily Job Campaign Calendar is designed to help you make things happen every day. To get maximum benefit from it:

- First, prepare three to five daily calendars with items from your Job Campaign Plan (see Part Three, "Planning Your Job Campaign").

- On each day, fill in future calendars as you progress. For example, if a contact says, "call me back in three weeks," start your calendar for that day with that instruction for yourself.

- Check off each item as it is completed.

- At the end of each day, evaluate your progress and complete your calendar for the next day.

- When you obtain a referral or complete an appointment, write your follow-up actions on your calendar.

- Reproduce your Daily Job Campaign Calendar forms and place them in your Career Starter notebook for convenience and effective follow-up.

## Daily Job Campaign Calendar

*Date* _____ *Day of Week* _____

***Appointments and Interviews*** (Enter into Networking Directory, Action Log and Job Prospect Profile; see pages 55, 73 and 90-91.)

| *Name* | *Location* | *Time* |
| --- | --- | --- |
| | | |
| | | |
| | | |

***Phone Calls*** (Enter into appropriate form, see above.)

| *Name* | *Telephone Number* |
| --- | --- |
| | |
| | |
| | |
| | |

***New Referrals*** (Enter into Networking Directory.)

| *Name* | *Telephone Number* |
| --- | --- |
| | |
| | |
| | |
| | |

***Resumés to Mail*** (Enter into Action Log.)

| *Name* | *Organization* |
| --- | --- |
| | |
| | |
| | |
| | |

***Follow-Up Letters and Thank-You Notes to Mail***
(Enter into Networking Directory or Action Log.)

| *Name* | *Organization* |
| --- | --- |
| | |
| | |
| | |
| | |

# ORGANIZING YOUR INFORMATION SOURCES

*First lady Hillary Rodham Clinton earned her undergraduate degree in political science from Wellesley College, in Wellesley, Mass., and her law degree from Yale.*

In this information age, the key issues in a job campaign are:

- What do I need?
- Where is it available?
- How do I use it?

This part of your *Career Starter* answers these questions and shows you how to get the information you need promptly, efficiently and inexpensively. We focus on six sources of job campaign information:

- Campus Career Services
- The Public Library
- Electronic Information Services
- Trade and Professional Associations
- Personnel Search Firms
- Your Personal Network

# CAMPUS CAREER SERVICES
(An Often Overlooked Resource)

Most colleges and universities offer a wide range of career- and job-search services to develop career-planning skills, teach job-search techniques and arrange contacts between students and employees. Typically, these services include:

- **Career Resource Library**
  Information including career guides, job descriptions, salary surveys, videotapes, employer information, and graduate and vocational training program catalogs are available in most centers.

- **Job Listings**
  Information about full-time or part-time jobs, summer jobs and internships may be available in print, or via computer or touchtone-telephone access.

- **Workshops**
  Some campuses have regularly scheduled career planning and job search workshops.

- **Consulting Services**
  Career consultants may be available to discuss career- and job-search issues. They may include services such as critiques of resumés and evaluations of videotaped practice interviews.

- **Job Fairs**
  Employers representing various organizations set up booths in one location to talk personally about job prospects. Many job fairs are sponsored by consortia of colleges or professional organizations.

- **Campus Interviews**
  Employers visit the campus each year to conduct preliminary interviews. This is a great way to gain interview experience.

- **Alumni Office**
  Some alumni offices offer referral services or lists of alumni whom you might contact. Check the Alumni Directory for possible networking contacts in your location of choice.

*Clint Eastwood, actor, film producer and director, dropped out of the business administration program at Los Angeles College.*

# THE PUBLIC LIBRARY
(A Gold Mine)

The public library is one of the most underrated resources for job-hunting. It is a gold mine of information. Here is a sample of what is available in print.

## Surveying the Field
- *American Almanac of Jobs & Salaries*
- *Occupational Outlook Handbook*
- *U.S. Industrial Outlook*
- *Dictionary of Occupational Titles*

## State and County
- State Industrial Directory
- County Directory of Business
- Local Chamber of Commerce Directory
- *MacRae's State Industrial Directory*
- Statewide Job Opportunities
- County Job List
- Interstate Job Bank

## Large Companies
- *Standard & Poor's Register of Corporations*
- *Dunn & Bradstreet Million Dollar Directory*
- *Moody's Industrial Manual*
- *Value Line Investment Survey*
- *CPC Placement Annual*

## Federal Government
- *Federal Career Opportunities*
- *U.S. Government Manual*
- *How to Get a Federal Job*
- *171 Reference Book (Government Job Application)*

## International
- *The Complete Guide to International Jobs*
- *The Almanac of International Jobs and Careers*
- *How to Get a Job in Europe*
- *Directory of Overseas Summer Jobs*
- *Guide to Careers in World Affairs*
- *European Markets*
- *International Careers*

## Specialty Publications
- *Directory of Directories*
- *Association Directories*
- *Business to Business Yellow Pages*
- *Peterson's Guides*
- *Directory of Executive Recruiters*
- *Worldwide Chamber of Commerce Directory*

## Newsletters
- *Career Opportunities News*
- *Career Waves*
- *Kennedy's Career Strategist*

## Periodicals
- *BusinessWeek*
- *Working Woman*
- *The Chronicle of Higher Education*
- *Federal Career Opportunities*
- *National Business Employment Weekly*

Spend a day at the library discovering these publications. The more you explore on your own, the more information you will turn up. It doesn't hurt to make the reference librarian your best friend; he or she can uncover valuable resources and leads you may not find on your own.

# ELECTRONIC INFORMATION SERVICES
(Welcome to the Twenty-First Century)

**A** number of information services allow you to access corporate information about a company, service, discipline, college or university via a personal computer. The primary advantage is speed. The main disadvantage is cost.

## On Your Own Computer

However, here are two low-cost after-hours services available directly to you via your own computer or indirectly through reference libraries or career resource centers.

- **After Dark**
  BRS Information Technologies, (800) 227-5277
  After Dark has some 150 databases offering information about business, education, social sciences, humanities, health, science and technology at reduced rates during evenings and weekends. A catalog of databases is available.

- **Knowledge Index**
  DIALOG Information Services, Inc., (800) 334-2564
  Knowledge Index is an evening and weekend service offering over one hundred databases covering business, technical and general interest subjects. It is designed for students and home computer users. A catalog of databases is available.

If you have a personal computer and modem, call the customer service numbers above for detailed information. If you don't, find out what type of online services are available at your college reference library, career center or local library.

*Between 1983 and 1990, the number of college graduates working as housekeepers, janitors and cleaners rose from 72,000 to 83,000. The number working as motor vehicle operators (mostly truck and bus drivers) rose from 99,000 to 166,000.*

## *If You Don't Own Your Own*

Some libraries have workstations available for students to use without a fee. Others may have only one or two stations and charge a fee. Sometimes reference libraries may accept search topics and a cost ceiling. They will then complete the search and charge the student for the actual charges incurred within the budgeted amount.

Most of the databases available online are also found on CD-ROM. There is little or no cost involved because the library purchases the system and subscribes to monthly updates. One disadvantage with CD-ROM is that the information can be outdated. Check with your library regarding the availability and timeliness of their CD-ROM databases.

*A Special Note:* If you are proficient in performing online searches, you already have an important job skill. Law firms, consulting firms, trade associations and various information services hire people who know how to conduct library research using electronic databases. Examples of such employers include BRS on the East Coast and Dialog on the West Coast.

# TRADE AND PROFESSIONAL ASSOCIATIONS
(A Trade Secret)

**M**ore than 50% of all new jobs come from the more than 13,500,000 small businesses in the U.S. Many of these small businesses belong to trade and professional associations. There now exists an association for practically every type of business or industry. It makes sense, then, that associations are an ideal source of information and contacts regarding the industry, companies and people they represent.

Trade associations are non-profit, cooperative, voluntary organizations of competitors in the same industry. They combine financial and human resources to deal with mutual business interests and problems, such as government regulations, industry statistics, standardization, international trade, and legal and accounting issues. An association may have a staff of one person or hundreds of people.

Almost all associations maintain a membership directory. These directories are often available free or for a minimal price. In addition, they may also publish newsletters, books, magazines, surveys and reports that will help you do your homework on a company or an industry.

One problem facing most growing industries today is a shortage of knowledgeable people. For them, career development is a high priority. Many of these associations provide catalogs or listings of career materials and programs. Catalogs may include recruitment brochures, scholarship pamphlets, industry reports, education programs, tapes, films and videos, and career placement information.

Some associations also operate a job referral service. The service may consist of newsletter listings, a computer database or a formal referral service. Even if a referral service does not exist, the trade association

*Business growth and upgrading is expected to create nearly 22% fewer jobs between 1990 and 2005 than it created between 1984 and 1990.*

personnel can be a valuable network resource. They can be very effective in directing you to the right people and places.

When calling an association, ask whether it has an employment referral service or career resource center. This may take persistence. Make sure you speak to a staff person who can help you get the information you want and be sure to explain exactly who you are and why you're calling. Ask for membership directories, education and training materials, special reports and referrals to specific leaders in your geographic area.

Association directories may be found in most libraries. They provide association names, addresses and phone numbers, membership information and descriptions of associations' missions. The following association directories collectively offer more than 10,000 listings:

- *Ayer's Association Directory*
- *Gale Global Access: Encyclopedia of Associations*
- *National Trade and Professional Associations*

# PERSONNEL SEARCH FIRMS
(What They Can and Cannot Do for You)

**F**irms that assist employers in finding job candidates are referred to by many names, such as search firms, personnel consultants, executive recruiters, employment agencies or headhunters. They come in two varieties: those whose fees are paid by employers and those whose fees are paid by job candidates.

## Fees Paid By Company

- **Retained Search**
  The search firm is retained on an exclusive basis, and the fee is paid regardless of the results of the search. Typically, this approach is for executive-level talent, not recent graduates.
- **Contingency Search**
  The fee is paid only if the candidate referred by the search firm is hired. This speculative approach may be appropriate for graduates with specific skills in demand by the workplace. Sometimes the newly hired person must promise to stay with the firm at least six months. If he or she doesn't stay, the search firm must reimburse the employer a prorated portion of the fee. Sometimes the employer will try to recover the cost from the employee.

## Fees Paid By Job Candidate

- **Contingency Placement**
  The candidate pays the fee only if he or she accepts the position. Many times, a contingency firm hunts for resumés to broadcast locally. Most firms hiring young professionals would rather hire directly than pay a fee to contingency recruiters. Beware of high pressure tactics used to get you to take a job that may not be what you want. Read the fine print and never prepay any fee.

*By the year 2005, only 20% to 25% of all jobs will require a bachelor's degree—but 30% of all workers will have one.*

*Jeff Smith, TV's "Frugal Gourmet," earned a bachelor's degree in philosophy and sociology at the University of Puget Sound in Tacoma, Wash., and then a master's of divinity from Drew Theological School in Madison, N.J.*

*William Hurt, actor, has a bachelor's degree in theology from Tufts University.*

- **Employment Services**
  Career evaluations, resumé preparation and practice interviewing services are offered to job candidates for a fee. Always ask for references, work samples and the opportunity to meet the person who will work on your behalf.

You must be extremely careful to use only highly reputable contingency firms. Ask for references and check each one out. Does the search firm belong to a professional association? Is it certified? Some less-professional firms may, in addition to pressuring you to take a job you don't want, present your credentials to many companies indiscriminately in order to obtain a fee. On the other hand, there are many reputable agencies with established company relationships and valuable industry contacts. Use professional and trade associations to find those agencies that may increase your chances of getting the right job. They may also give you helpful counseling, interview tips, career ideas and resumé help.

## A Final Word

Always call a search firm prior to writing a letter. Most letters from inexperienced candidates are ignored. Handle the call similarly to a call for any information interview (see page 53). If you are asked to send a resumé, make sure your cover letter is addressed to the person with whom you spoke. Always follow up to make sure the person has received it and to determine the next step.

## Suggested Reading

- *The Directory of Executive Recruiters*
  Kennedy Publications, Fitzwilliam, NH
  (603) 585-6544

# YOUR PROFESSIONAL NETWORK
("Know Who" Versus "Know How")

**N**etworking is the cultivation and use of personal contacts to exchange information. In a job campaign you need information regarding careers, companies, jobs and people. The best sources for this information are personal contacts.

## Why Use Networking?

- Between 60% and 70% of all jobs are filled through networking.

- One-on-one contact is the most effective way to get yourself hired.

- You can learn about unpublished job requirements before your competition does.

- You gain a competitive edge by being referred directly to a potential employer rather than by being processed through a recruiting system.

## How to Network

Networking is easier than you think. You already have a social network (relatives, personal friends, classmates, etc.). Now you need to expand your personal network into a job campaign network. Remember, everyone who has a job has been in your situation, and most successful people are willing to help. Here is how to develop your job campaign network.

1. **Get organized.** Keep track of every contact. Look at the Networking Directory form on page 55. It provides the means to create your own personal networking directory. Update your directory daily.

*Joseph Wapner, TV personality ("Peoples' Court") and retired judge, earned a bachelor's degree in philosophy at the University of Southern California.*

*Lou Reed, musician and songwriter, earned a bachelor's degree in English with a minor in modern philosophy from Syracuse University.*

*First Jobs: Pee-wee Herman, comedian, was a busboy, prep-man in a pizza parlor, sandwich dresser in a fast-food restaurant and a Fuller Brush salesman.*

2. **Get the word out that you are searching for a job.** Ask friends, relatives, professors and people who graduated last year about opportunities where they work. Contact people you know who work for firms where you would like to work. Ask for leads and referrals. Try to obtain at least two or three names from each person.

3. **Contact trade and professional organizations for job banks, membership directories, newsletter listings, etc.** Obtain lists of company contacts from college placement offices. Get lists of established professionals from college alumni offices.

4. **Target individuals in a field or company you would like to get into and ask for an information (not a job) interview.** Call key people whose names you have obtained and ask for an appointment to learn more about their specific industry. You will be surprised how effective this approach is. People are flattered to be asked for advice. In addition, they will usually give you names of friends, acquaintances and firms to call as well as ideas for you to try.

    When calling to schedule an information interview, remember to:

    - Introduce yourself.

    - If you have been referred, give that person's name.

    - State that you are requesting an appointment for a 30-minute information interview.

    - Ask to arrange a mutually convenient time.

## *Tips for Successful Networking*

- Script what you are going to say on the phone (see Part Six, pages 78-79).

- Ask a secretary for assistance getting to the person you are calling. If this doesn't work, call before 8:30 A.M. or after 5:30 P.M., when the person is more likely to answer his or her own phone, or leave a message in their voice mailbox (see page 81).

- If the person has voice mail, leave a message containing the information described above. For example, you could call the targeted individual and say:

  *"Hello, my name is Virginia Union and I was referred to you by Cary Collins. I'm interested in the public relations industry. I'm calling to ask if you might have thirty minutes to meet me. I'm looking for information on the various aspects of the industry and some advice on how to become a part of it."*

- If the person's answer is "yes," say,

  *"When would it be convenient to meet?"*

- If the answer is negative, say,

  *"Could you recommend someone else I could call?"*

- Then thank your contact for his or her interest and kindness.

**First Job: Bryant Gumbel, broadcast journalist, was a sales representative for a paper bag and folding carton manufacturer.**

## Electronic Networking

For those of you who have a personal computer and modem, you may have the ability to network electronically via computer networks such as CompuServe, Internet, BITNET, Usenet, MCI Mail, Prodigy, Genie, and America On-Line. The advantage of these services is that they allow you to send messages and post announcements on electronic bulletin boards around the world. In addition, there are all kinds of network groups that you may participate in to explore job opportunities, submit resumés and join on-line conferences with other users who are working in your area of interest. These services provide opportunities to find out about the issues, concerns and interests of the people whose field you're exploring or hope to join.

## Suggested Reading

- *Information Interviewing:*
  *What It Is and How to Use It in Your Career*
  Martha Stoodley, Garrett Park Press

- *The Complete Handbook of Personal*
  *Computer Communications*
  Alfred Glossbrenner, St. Martin's Press

## Conducting an Information Interview

The objectives of an information interview are to learn more about a field and to obtain contacts for job opportunities. This referral information is the key to getting results.

### The Questions to Ask

1. How did you get started in this business?

2. What are the positive aspects of being in this business?

3. If you had to do it again, what would you do differently?

4. Where do you see the industry heading now and in the future?

5. What and where are the current career opportunities in the industry?

6. Is there a trade association representing the industry?

7. Is there someone with the association I should talk with?

8. Who would you recommend I contact regarding job opportunities?

9. Is there anything else I should know about the industry?

10. What would you do if you were in my situation?

### Some Helpful Hints

- Relax, this is not a job interview—it will be fun.

- Prepare questions in advance and take notes.

- Bring a resumé and ask for comments, suggestions, ideas.

- Ask for referrals to other people in the career field.

- Leave your resumé for possible follow-up.

- Send a thank-you note, and keep the person posted on your progress.

- Update your Networking Directory every day.

# HOW TO USE YOUR NETWORKING DIRECTORY

The following work sheet will help you keep track of your personal network of contacts. Reproduce one of these two-page forms for each letter of the alphabet (mark them A through Z) and place them in your *Career Starter* notebook to produce your own Networking Directory.

Record the date of the telephone call/meeting, the person's name, title, company, address and phone numbers, who they were referred by, who they referred you to, and when you sent a thank-you letter. Use as many blocks as you need to accommodate all the information.

You may also want to place notes of conversations with your networking contacts in your *Career Starter* notebook. Label each set of notes with the person's name, address and phone number, and file them alphabetically (by the first initial of each last name) after the appropriate networking directory work sheet. Or, you could also create a folder for each networking contact.

If you learn that a networking contact has a job to offer, reenter that information in the Action Log (see page 73) and on a Job Prospect Profile (see page 90).

Your Networking Directory will serve as a permanent record for continuing use during your career. You will find it a valuable reference if your keep it current as time passes.

COPY

## Networking Directory

| Date of Contact | Person's Name and Title | Telephone Number | Company's Name and Address | Date of Thank You | Referred By | Provided Referrals To |
|---|---|---|---|---|---|---|
| | | | | | | |
| | | | | | | |
| | | | | | | |
| | | | | | | |
| | | | | | | |
| | | | | | | |
| | | | | | | |
| | | | | | | |

PART

FIVE

# WHEN YOU'RE MARKETING YOURSELF

# THE MARKETING PROCESS

**A** job campaign involves marketing, whether we recognize it or not. Marketing is a process that provides all the supporting resources to sell a product or service. In a job campaign, you are the product. You must market yourself to the prospective employer. That means making sure that he or she clearly understands your ability to serve the organization's needs. Given that measurement of success, let's see how you can market yourself. The marketing process consists of these four functions:

- **Presentation**
  Offering your skills and experience as beneficial to the prospective employer.

- **Promotion**
  Creating awareness of your capabilities.

- **Positioning**
  Gaining a preference or competitive advantage.

- **Pricing**
  Getting what you are worth in today's market.

## Action Words to Make Your Point

| | |
|---|---|
| Achieve | Market |
| Analyze | Monitor |
| Attain | Motivate |
| Calculate | Negotiate |
| Coach | Obtain |
| Compose | Organize |
| Conduct | Originate |
| Contribute | Plan |
| Create | Prepare |
| Design | Present |
| Develop | Produce |
| Direct | Promote |
| Enhance | Propose |
| Evaluate | Recommend |
| Expedite | Research |
| Forecast | Resolve |
| Generate | Schedule |
| Identify | Sell |
| Improve | Simplify |
| Initiate | Specify |
| Install | Start |
| Instruct | Supervise |
| Integrate | Teach |
| Interview | Train |
| Investigate | Translate |
| Make | Write |

# PRESENTATION
(You Are What Your Resumé Says You Are)

Your resumé presents your qualifications to a prospective employer. It must convince him or her that you are a qualified candidate. Its objective is to get you an interview. Your resumé should:

- Highlight the benefits you offer.

- Show how your capabilities satisfy the employer's requirements.

- Differentiate you from the crowd by emphasizing your accomplishments.

## The Contents

- **Best Approach**
  Try to obtain a copy of a job description and tailor your resumé to the specific job requirements. This is easy if you have access to a personal computer and a laser printer. Otherwise, go with a generic resumé.

- **Objective**
  Your job objective may be stated in your resumé or in your cover letter. Regardless, your objective should adhere to the following formula. Describe the type of position you want, the type of organization you want to work in or the area of interest you want to pursue, the skills you want to use, and any experience that you want to highlight.

- **Education**
  List the names of educational institutions, degrees, dates awarded, honors and awards (GPA if 3.5 or above), and the percentage of educational costs that were paid through grants, scholarships, jobs, cooperatives, and student loans.

- **Skills**
  Match your skills to the specific job requirements, consistent with your job objective.

- **Experience**
  Focus on your ABCs:

    *Accomplishments*
    Activities with tangible results.

    *Benefits*
    How you satisfy the specific needs of the potential employer.

    *Capabilities*
    What you can produce or deliver.

## *Language*

Write in the first person without the pronoun "I." For example, use "produced" rather than "I produced."

Use action verbs such as "achieve" (if you're referring to your current job), "achieved" (if referring to a previous job). The accompanying list may help you find the right words.

Avoid referring to activities, duties and responsibilities. Replace with your ABCs discussed earlier.

Be brief, accurate and focused.

In 1992,
Turi Josefsen,
executive vice
president of U.S.
Surgical Corp., was
the highest-paid
woman in corporate
America earning
$23.6 million
including stock
options. She was
also the best-paid
among all corporate
executives below
the level of CEO.
Ms. Josefsen
doesn't have a
college degree.

## Design

The key is to present your skills and experience as effectively as possible, depending on who you are trying to impress. For starters, your resumé should look like a published document—uncluttered with plenty of white space.

Three resumé formats—*chronological, functional* and a *combined chronological/functional*—are presented in this book for your consideration (see pages 64-66). The chronological format is probably the most widely used and most recognizable format. It allows the reader to find pertinent information quickly and effectively. You'll want to use a functional format if you don't already have work experience. You'll be able to concentrate on your skills rather than your experience, and you won't jeopardize your position as a job candidate. The combination of these formats highlights your job experiences and the skills you have gained in these positions.

Regardless of format, use just one page. More detailed information can be provided during the interview. Later on in your career, when you have gained more experience, your resumé can be longer.

## Administrative Details

Ask a placement or personnel professional to critique your resumé and suggest appropriate improvements.

If you use a personal computer to tailor your resumé to specific job requirements, be sure to use a laser printer to produce the best quality. If you don't have a laser printer, take your resumé on diskette to someone who does.

If you use a generic resumé, have it professionally printed on good quality paper. Your printer can advise you on the proper choice and colors of paper. Generally, you will want a heavy, high-quality paper in natural white, ivory, light almond or light grey. Request at least 200 to 300 copies of your resumé. It is not cost-effective to print under 100.

Always send your resumé with a cover letter tailored to the particular job. It should be sent to the specific person (name and title) in the company responsible for hiring you.

Always send your resumé in a large envelope so it does not get folded.

## Suggested Reading

- *From College to Career:*
  *Entry-Level Resumés for Any Major*
  Donald Asher, Ten Speed Press

- *Resumés That Knock 'Em Dead*
  Martin John Yate, Bob Adams, Inc.

## Suggested Software

- *ResuméMaker*
  Individual Software, Inc.

- *The Resumé Kit*
  Spinnaker Software Corporation

**William Gates, co-founder and CEO of Microsoft, dropped out of pre-law at Harvard at the end of his sophomore year.**

## Common Resumé Mistakes to Avoid

*Make sure your resumé doesn't include:*

- Misspelled words.

- Typographical errors.

- Sloppy grammar or syntax.

- Confused chronology.

- Your current or previous salaries.

- Personal data (age, marital status).

- Reference to health conditions.

- Religious or political affiliations.

- Names of references.

*Make sure your resumé does:*

- Make it easy for someone to get a quick assessment of your skills.

- Include succinct descriptions.

- Emphasize your most significant skills and accomplishments in a prominent position.

## Resumé Checklist

The following checklist has been designed to assist you in evaluating your resumé. Make sure your resumé meets the following criteria. (Go through this checklist each time you change your resumé.)

### 1. Appearance
❏ is visually pleasing
❏ is easy to read
❏ looks like a published document

### 2. Contact Information
❏ is clearly presented at top
❏ includes current address
❏ includes telephone number(s) where you can be reached during business hours (9 A.M. to 5 P.M.)

### 3. Objective
❏ includes type of job you seek
❏ includes type of organization
❏ emphasizes your strongest skills

### 4. Education
❏ lists most recent degree; date or anticipated date of graduation
❏ lists other relevant education certificate programs, short courses
❏ includes name and location of university, college or training institution
❏ names major, minor and/or area(s) of concentration or interest
❏ lists honors and awards
❏ mentions GPA if 3.5 or above
❏ tells percentage of education you paid through jobs, grants, scholarships and student loans

### 5. Skills
❏ are consistent with objective
❏ should match job requirements
❏ are substantiated by experience

### 6. Experience
Each paid, volunteer, intern, or co-op experience relevant to your objective that you list includes:
❏ title, organization name, city, state and/or country (if not U.S.)
❏ dates position held
❏ position description that highlights skills, relevant accomplishments and benefits you offer
❏ specific examples of successes to substantiate your objective

### 7. Extracurricular Activities
❏ list offices held, including title and organization
❏ emphasize leadership roles
❏ include pertinent memberships and affiliations
❏ include sports participation
❏ list ROTC training
❏ present certifications, such as those for paralegal, emergency medical technician or lifesaving
❏ include significant class papers, relevant conferences attended and foreign study/language fluency

## Sample Resumé—Chronological Format

### Virginia C. Union
2323 Sullivan Ballou Avenue, Bull Run, Virginia 22090, Phone (703) 555-1234

**Objective**   Obtain a position as a writer with a public relations firm utilizing my degree in English, my word processing and desktop publishing skills, and my staff writing experience.

**Education**   **Virginia Commonwealth University,** Richmond, Virginia, Bachelor of Arts in English, May 1992, *cum laude.* GPA: 3.5. Fifty percent of education paid through scholarships, jobs, student loans and internships. Honors include Dean's List and Lee Foundation scholarship.

**Skills**
- Excellent research, interviewing, writing and editorial skills.
- Meet deadlines. Obtain quality results working with other people.
- Proficiency in Macintosh Microsoft Word, Pagemaker 4.0 and Freehand 2.0, and BRS and Dialog information services.

**Experience**   **Staff Writer,** Environmental Services, Inc., Washington, D.C., July 1992–Present.
Research and write proposals and project reports for submittal to the U.S. Environmental Protection Agency.

**Campus Correspondent,** *The Richmond News Leader,* Richmond, Virginia, August 1990–May 1992.
Wrote feature articles for the Young Virginians section.

**Staff Writer**, *New Age for Seniors,* Richmond, Virginia, January 1990–January 1992.
Wrote feature articles and calendar of events. Helped plan monthly issues. Typeset editorial and ad copy. Distributed subscription orders.

**Assistant Editor**, Telecon Database Marketing Company, Cedar Rapids, Iowa, June 1988–August 1988.
Coordinated a staff of volunteer reporters; wrote, edited, designed and distributed internal company newsletter.

**References**   Available upon request.

## Sample Resumé—Functional Format

*Virginia C. Union*
*2323 Sullivan Ballou Avenue, Bull Run, Virginia 22090, Phone (703) 555-1234*

**Objective**

Obtain a position as a writer with a public relations firm utilizing my degree in English, my word processing and desktop publishing skills, and my staff writing experience.

**Education**

Virginia Commonwealth University, Richmond, Virginia, Bachelor of Arts in English, May 1992, *cum laude.* GPA: 3.5. Fifty percent of education paid through scholarships, jobs, student loans and internships. Honors include Dean's List and Lee Foundation scholarship.

**Skills**

- Excellent research, interviewing, writing and editorial skills.
- Proficiency using BRS and Dialog electronic information services.
- Meet deadlines. Obtain quality results working with other people.

**Experience**

**Research.** Currently perform library and computer on-line information searches for own use in writing proposals and technical reports for environmental services firm.

**Interviewing.** Conducted more than one hundred personal interviews with students, educators, professionals and business representatives as campus correspondent for Richmond, Virginia newspaper. Obtains desired results with pleasant personality, open mind and quick thinking.

**Writing.** Wrote more than 250 feature and news articles, newsletters, proposals and reports as staff writer and newspaper intern reporter. Writing samples available upon request.

**Editorial Services/Desktop Publishing.** Published internal company newsletter utilizing a staff of summer volunteer reporters. Managed editing, layout, design and distribution as Assistant Editor. Used Macintosh Microsoft Word, Pagemaker 4.0 and Freehand 2.0.

**References**

Available upon request.

## Sample Resumé—Combined Chronological and Functional Format

*Virginia C. Union*
*2323 Sullivan Ballou Avenue, Bull Run, Virginia 22090, Phone (703) 555-1234*

**Objective**   Obtain a position as a writer with a public relations firm utilizing my degree in English, my word processing and desktop publishing skills, and my staff writing experience.

**Education**   **Virginia Commonwealth University,** Richmond, Virginia, Bachelor of Arts in English, May 1992, *cum laude*. GPA: 3.5. Fifty percent of education paid through scholarships, jobs, student loans and internships. Honors include Dean's List and Lee Foundation scholarship.

**Skills**   • Excellent research, interviewing, writing and editorial skills.
• Proficiency using BRS and Dialog electronic information services.
• Meet deadlines. Obtain quality results working with other people.

**Accomplishments**

**Interviewing**. Conducted more than one hundred personal interviews with professionals, students, educators and business leaders as campus correspondent for Richmond, VA, newspaper.

**Writing.** Wrote more than 250 feature and news articles, newsletters, proposals and reports as staff writer and newspaper intern reporter. Writing samples available upon request.

**Word Processing/Desktop Publishing.** Produced more than 200 pages of documents using Macintosh Microsoft Word, Pagemaker 4.0 and Freehand 2.0.

**Experience**   **Staff Writer,** Environmental Services, Inc., Washington, DC, July 1992–Present.

**Campus Correspondent,** *The Richmond News Leader,* Richmond, VA, Aug. 1990–May 1992.

**Staff Writer,** *New Age for Seniors,* Richmond, VA, Jan. 1990–Jan. 1992.

**Assistant Editor,** Telecon Database Marketing Company, Cedar Rapids, IA, June–Aug. 1988.

**References**   Available upon request.

# RESUMÉ COVER LETTERS

**A** cover letter serves as an introduction to your resumé and an opportunity to say something specific about how you qualify for the specific job. Organize your letter as follows:

- **Paragraph 1**
  State objective, benefits you can provide and the source of your referral.

- **Paragraph 2**
  Indicate why you are interested in the position, how you are qualified for it and why the company (or job if known) appeals to you.

- **Paragraph 3**
  Request a specific form of response, state your next step and thank the reader for his or her time and consideration.

The sample cover letter on the next page illustrates the recommended approach.

## Sample Resumé Cover Letter

**Virginia C. Union**
**2323 Sullivan Ballou Avenue**
**Bull Run, Virginia  22090**
**(703) 555-1234**

July 1, 1993

Ms. Jill Senate
Director of Communications
Washington Associates, Inc.
1801 Pennsylvania Avenue, N.W.
Washington, DC  20000

Dear Ms. Senate:

I would like to explore the possibility of joining your organization as a staff writer. My degree in English, word processing skills and staff writing experience qualify me for such a position. I was referred to you by Ms. Jane Wilson of the Public Relations Society of America.

I am seeking a position that will utilize and expand my writing skills. My specific experience in writing proposals and reports for the U.S. Environmental Protection Agency should be of interest since your clients include chemical manufacturers. Also, my work in the environmental field fits your organization's work with the petroleum industry.

My resumé summarizes my qualifications. In addition, I would appreciate the opportunity to discuss with you in more detail how I can assist your organization. I will call you the week of July 12th to arrange an appointment. In the meantime, thank you for your consideration of my qualifications.

Sincerely,


Virginia C. Union
Enclosure

# PROMOTION
(Getting Noticed)

**P**romotion is making an audience of potential employers aware of your qualifications. Here are six nontraditional ways to accomplish this task:

**1.** You can use electronic resumé services such as KiNexus, (312) 335-0787, to broadcast your resumé.

**2.** List yourself in appropriate trade association newsletters under "Positions Wanted." (See page 45.)

**3.** Prepare 3 x 5 or rotary file (i.e., Rolodex) "leave behind" cards that contain your name, address and phone number on the front and your job objective and skills from your resumé on the back. You can get these printed by most printers. Carry some with you at all times, and give one to anyone who may have reason to contact you later about a job.

**4.** Be your own working advertisement by working as a temp. A temporary job as a clerk, receptionist or courier provides valuable experiences, contacts and references. Sometimes the temporary job will lead directly to a permanent position.

**5.** Volunteer for organizations and activities with business sponsors or relationships. This will increase your visibility and personal contacts.

**6.** Participate actively in your college alumni association. If an employer has had success with graduates of your college, you start off with a positive perception. And alumni can refer you to their customers, vendors and competitors.

Additional promotional approaches are discussed in Part Six, "Job Campaign Tactics That Work."

# POSITIONING
(Preparation Finding Opportunity)

**In 1992, of all graduate students, MBAs with technical undergraduate degrees and more than four years of experience were offered the highest average salary— $56,298.**

Positioning (also known as networking) is arranging to be known in the right place at the right time when a job opportunity develops. How can you do this? Here is a proven approach for strategic career positioning:

• **Join a club** that has a business/educational orientation rather than a pure social function. Every profession has such an organization. Many have student memberships. Check with the appropriate trade association to find a club in your area.

• **Participate in the club's activities.** Volunteer to be on a committee. View the time as an investment in your future career.

• **Be patient.** You probably won't land a job from the first meeting. It takes time to build rapport and respect with the other members. Above all, don't oversell yourself. Just work hard for the mutual benefit of all the club members.

• **Maintain reasonable expectations.** The rewards will come in small packages. The one great job opportunity may come after a series of little learning experiences. But it will be worth it.

• **Send thank-you notes for any assistance you receive.** It's amazing how few people do this. Yet, it always makes a good impression. Guess whose name is going to pop into someone's mind when a job opportunity does arise?

Additional approaches to gain a competitive advantage are discussed in Part Six, "Job Campaign Tactics That Work."

## PRICING
(Dollars and Sense)

**W**hat you will be offered for your services will depend upon the ability/resources of the employer, your qualifications, the job salary range, location and current market conditions. To get some idea of what different jobs pay, you can obtain salary data from the following sources:

- Trade and professional association surveys

- *College Placement Council Salary Survey*

- *America Almanac of Jobs and Salaries*

- Professionals in the career field

- Previous year's graduates

The next step is to develop a monthly expense budget to see how much gross income you will need to live. This will depend on where you live and your spending habits. Estimate your take-home pay to be approximately 65% of your gross pay. Be sure to include a reserve for the inevitable emergencies. Then compare your needs with published salary ranges to determine your personal salary requirements.

Salary negotiations are discussed in Part Seven, "Interviewing For First Place." Surviving on your income is discussed in Part Three, "Planning Your Job Campaign."

*Of all graduate students, candidates for master's degrees in journalism received the lowest average salary offer—$22,699.*

# How to Use Your Action Log

**U**se this Action Log to track your contacts with prospective employers and the dates of your correspondence, phone calls and interviews with them. Be as detailed and organized as possible—it will make your follow-up easier and more effective.

Reproduce this form for each letter of the alphabet (mark them "A" through "Z") and place them in your *Career Starter* notebook. You may wish to file your Job Prospect Profile work sheets alphabetically (by the first initial of each person's last name) after the appropriate Action Log sheet.

## Action Log

| Name of Company, Name of Contact and Telephone Number | Dates Resumés Sent | Dates of Telephone Calls | Dates Correspondence Sent | Dates of Interviews |
|---|---|---|---|---|
| | | | | |
| | | | | |
| | | | | |
| | | | | |
| | | | | |
| | | | | |
| | | | | |
| | | | | |
| | | | | |
| | | | | |
| | | | | |
| | | | | |
| | | | | |
| | | | | |
| | | | | |
| | | | | |

# JOB CAMPAIGN TACTICS THAT WORK

# THE PRINCIPLES OF SUCCESS

View your job campaign as an opportunity to meet different people, learn new skills and experience new adventures. The result will be an exciting and rewarding experience. Enjoy the process of becoming a wiser person.

Your job campaign strategy is the big picture, and it focuses your efforts toward your career goal. Your job campaign tactics are the day-to-day actions that produce the results. Which is more important: strategy or tactics? Both. It's the combination of the two that will make your job campaign successful. Make day-to-day adjustments to your game plan. You will write the script as you move ahead.

The job campaign tactics presented in this part of *Career Starter* are proven techniques designed to help you outwit and outmaneuver your competition. However, it is up to you to outwork your competitors to get the job you want. In addition, you may want to keep the following principles in mind as you implement your job campaign tactics.

*The unemployment rate among college graduates was 6.9% in 1991, slightly more than the national unemployment rate for all workers (6.7%).*

## Compete To Win.

Only the winner gets the job. Never settle for average. Polish your job search skills every day. Improve your marketing materials as you learn. Always ask yourself, "How can I do it any better?" Then do it better.

## Maintain A Positive Attitude.

Rejection is normal when competing for a job. Do not let rejection lead to discouragement. Always obtain something of value from each call, contact or interview. Then build on each and every small victory. A series of small victories will increase your confidence and lead to ultimate success in your job campaign.

### Do Your Homework.

Preparation gives you a competitive edge. A display of intimate knowledge about an industry, a company, a job or the interviewer is crucial to getting the job you want. Invest the time to do the required research. It will pay dividends.

### Work Harder and Smarter Than Others.

There is no substitute for working *hard* and *smart*. Working hard turns up unexpected opportunities. Working smart eliminates time-wasting diversions. When in doubt, *act*. Do something simple, and then you can expand on it.

### Be Persistent.

Take full responsibility for getting the job you want, and never give up. One more phone call may lead to exactly the job opportunity you want. One more visit may produce an acquaintance who can help you. One more rejection letter may motivate you to change tactics for better results.

# COMMUNICATING TO GET RESULTS

## *The Telephone*

Next to face-to-face contact, the telephone is the most personal means available to find a job. Every call you make is an opportunity to talk with a prospective employer, to discover a new job opening or to obtain a referral. Your approach in the initial telephone contact can have a positive impact on your chances to obtain what you want from the call. Try these suggestions:

- Complete at least ten calls per day. You will be amazed at the results.

- Develop your own telephone personality, but always be pleasant, courteous and confident. Smile when you speak; the listener will hear it.

- Prepare a brief outline for each call and rehearse. Then relax, call and have a friendly conversation.

- Think in terms of short statements covering what you want to accomplish.

- Call around 8 A.M. and after 5 P.M. if you want to avoid secretaries.

- Get to know every secretary by name. He or she is the gate keeper who can assure or deny access to the person with whom you need to speak. Ask to receive information about the company (annual reports, newsletters, brochures) and, if possible, a copy of the job description.

- Voice mail is a great way to speak directly to the proper person. Use it to leave concise messages.

*Carol Burnett, actress and comedienne, dropped out of the theater and English program at the University of California at Los Angeles during her junior year.*

*Harry Connick, Jr., jazz musician and song writer, dropped out of the Manhattan School of Music during his junior year.*

- Take notes during each telephone conversation. If appropriate, attach the notes to the Job Prospect form in this section. Date all notes.

- If you get a negative response, ask for referrals to other people, companies or organizations.

- All calls have value. You just have to find it. Always ask for referrals . . . referrals . . . referrals.

## Telephone Inquiry Procedure for Success (TIPS)

### Objective

Use the telephone to arrange an information interview and to obtain leads.

### Finding the Right Person

If you don't have the name of a key executive in the area you wish to work, ask the receptionist for it. For example, what is the name of your General Manager? Vice President of Sales? Customer Service Director? Write it down, and then ask to speak with that person.

### Dealing With the Secretary

- Say: *"Hello, this is Virginia Union, may I speak with Mr. (Name)?"*

- If you are asked who you represent, say: *"Myself."*

- If you are asked about the subject of the call, say: *"I have been asked by (name of referral) to talk with Mr. (Name) about a personal matter."*

- If you are asked about the subject of the call and were not referred, just say: *"A personal matter."*

- If the executive is not available, leave your name and number for the person to return your call. And, be sure to get the name of the secretary so you can address him or her by name the next time you call.

- Note all calls in your Action Log for future reference or in your Networking Directory, if you're working in that stage of the game (see pages 55 and 73).

- If you are talking from your home, use a longer telephone cord. That way you can stand or move about, which may relieve initial anxiety. However, you may have to sit down to take notes.

- Use voice mail or an answering machine to receive messages while you are away from the phone.

### When You Reach Your Target

- Say: *"Hello, Ms. (Name), this is Virginia Union. I appreciate you talking with me today. I know you must receive many calls, so I'll be brief. I'm a recent graduate of Virginia Commonwealth University with a Bachelor's degree in English. My goal is to be a staff writer with a company such as yours taking advantage of my writing experience and desktop publishing skills. I'd appreciate the opportunity to talk with you about your requirements you might have to improve your corporate communications."*

- If the executive is hesitant, indicate that you will need only 20 minutes of time, that you will bring your resumé with you to save time and that you want to schedule the appointment at his or her convenience.

- If the executive wants to refer you to the personnel manager, ask if it is possible to meet with the executive first to obtain some background information.

- If the executive says there are no new positions available at this time, ask for an information interview or referrals. Say: *"Would it be possible to have an information interview to learn more about your industry?"* Or: *"Do you know of any of your associates who may need someone with my skills and experience?"*

- If nothing seems to be working, say: *"What do you suggest for someone in my situation?"*

- If you reach a complete dead end, smile, say: *"Thank you,"* and move on.

- Send an appropriate follow-up letter (see the following sample).

## Sample Phone Follow-Up Cover Letter

**Virginia C. Union**
**2323 Sullivan Ballou Avenue**
**Bull Run, Virginia  22090**
**(703) 555-1234**

July 10, 1993

Ms. Jill Senate
Director of Communications
Washington Associates, Inc.
1801 Pennsylvania Avenue, N.W.
Washington, DC  20000

Dear Ms. Senate:

Thank you for speaking with me on the phone today about my interest in joining your firm as staff writer. I have enclosed my resumé as you requested.

As we discussed, I am seeking a position in which I can utilize and expand my writing skills. My specific experience in writing proposals and reports to the U.S. Environmental Protection Agency should be of interest because your clients include chemical manufacturers. Also, my work in the environmental field fits your organization's business focus.

My resumé summarizes my qualifications. In addition, I would appreciate the opportunity to meet with you to discuss in more detail how I can assist your organization. I will call you the week of July 19th to arrange an appointment. In the meantime, thank you for your consideration of my qualifications.

Sincerely,


Virginia C. Union

Enclosure

### The Fax

In some cases, you may be asked to fax your resumé. In other situations, using a fax for delivery can get you special attention over other candidates. For example, you may want to fax your resumé in response to an ad and mail a printed copy at the same time. Always fax a cover letter with your resumé. And always call to confirm that the fax was received. Fax services are available in many office supply, packaging and quick-print stores.

### Voice Mail

Voice mail is a sophisticated telephone answering system that allows you to leave messages directly with the person you are calling without playing telephone tag or going through a secretary. Incoming touch-tone phone calls are directed to the recipient's voice mail box, where you hear a personalized greeting and are requested to leave a detailed message. This is a perfect opportunity to present your clear and concise message.

Sometimes, a fully automated system will ask you to input the extension of the person you are calling. If this is the case, wait for a live person to come on the line and ask for the person's extension. If you land in "voice mail jail," where you are cycled from one recorded message to another, call information and attempt to get a direct number.

Some colleges, universities and corporations offer voice mail job lines. These are recorded job listings with the actual voices of employers stating their specific job requirements. The services are available 24 hours a day, 7 days a week. If you are dealing with larger companies, trade associations or college career services, ask whether they have a voice mail job line.

*Sally Jesse Raphaël, daytime talk-show host, earned a bachelor of fine arts from Columbia University.*

## *Personal Cover Letters*

Most generic resumés accompanied by generic cover letters fail to get interviews. Cover letters and resumés usually don't get read beyond the first few lines, and the generic ones tend to get disqualified within 20 seconds. If you elect to use the cover letter approach, you should be prepared to do three things:

1. Persuade the reader to read your entire resumé and then talk with you by making your cover letter focused and to the point. (See Part Five, "When You're Marketing Yourself," for tips on presenting yourself and your correspondence effectively.)

2. Personalize your cover letter.

3. Follow up with a phone call within five days.

Also, keep in mind the following:

- A personal letter should be just that—a letter with a personal flavor. You want the reader to think he or she is getting the only copy of this letter, not a much-mailed form letter.

- Use simple, straightforward language to let the reader know what you want.

- Write in terms of how the reader will benefit from doing what you ask in the letter.

## Sample Personal Cover Letter (With Resumé)

**Virginia C. Union**
**2323 Sullivan Ballou Avenue**
**Bull Run, Virginia  22090**
**(703) 555-1234**

July 10, 1993

Ms. Jill Senate
Director of Communications
Washington Associates, Inc.
1801 Pennsylvania Avenue, N.W.
Washington, DC  20000

Dear Ms. Senate:

I would like to explore the possibility of joining your organization as a staff writer. My degree in English, word processing skills and staff writing experience qualify me for such a position.

I am seeking a position in which I can use and expand my writing skills. My specific experience in writing proposals and reports to the U.S. Environmental Protection Agency should be of interest because your clients include chemical manufacturers. Also, my work in the environmental field fits your organization's business focus.

My resumé summarizes my qualifications. In addition, I would appreciate the opportunity to meet with you and discuss in more detail how I can assist your organization. I will call you the week of July 19th to arrange an appointment. In the meantime, thank you for your consideration of my qualifications.

Sincerely,


Virginia C. Union

Enclosure

# ANSWERING ADVERTISEMENTS

*On average, in 1990 women with four or more years of college earned just over $30,000 while men with college educations earned about $43,000.*

In today's world, most business communications are via the telephone and fax. However, some of you may be more comfortable using the mail. And, sometimes you must send your response to a classified ad to a post office box. Even so, always try to follow up a letter with a phone call. Otherwise, you are probably wasting your time. Here are some guidelines that will enable you to get the most out of your mailings.

The key to success in responding to a classified ad is to separate yourself from the crowd by matching your qualifications to the ad's requirements. Some important job information will be presented in the ad itself. Now you need to:

- Call and find out as much as possible about the job, the company, and the qualifications of the person the company wants. Try to obtain a copy of the job description and the name of the hiring executive from the personnel manager.

- If you are told to "please send your resumé as directed," explain that you are just trying to respond effectively so you won't be wasting the personnel manager's time.

- Tailor your resumé and/or cover letter to the job requirements. Match the key words in the ad to your key qualifications.

- Write a cover letter that shows a special interest in or unique qualification for the job, and refer to your telephone conversation.

- Check your cover letter and resumé for mistakes. Then ask someone with an eye for detail to check it. Then check it again.

- Keep copies of all letters filed in your *Career Starter* notebook for quick and effective follow-up. Remember, cover letters are a good place to jot down notes or directions while you are on the phone.

- Call the hiring executive to give a "heads-up" that your resumé is coming. Use your telephone approach to get a commitment from the hiring executive to look specifically for your resumé and to send you a copy of the job description if you don't have it.

- If no corporate name is given (a "blind ad"), call the newspaper's classified section and ask for the name of the advertiser. Some states require that such information be furnished upon request.

*But, prior to 1986, men with high school diplomas earned more on average than women with college degrees.*

# USING MAILING LISTS

**S**hotgun mailings are a waste of time. The key to success is to target your audience. The more precise your target audience, the better your chance for results.

- Obtain lists of people by job function from trade association membership and other industry directories (see page 42).

- Check each list and eliminate companies you are not really interested in due to size, location, etc.

- Focus your mailings to the specific people in the companies you have targeted.

- Never mail a resumé to a company without an individual's name and title.

- Tailor your resumé and cover letter to address a precise job function in the targeted company.

- Use your Action Log (see page 73) for tracking your mailings.

## Delivery Services

Once in a while, you may require overnight letter delivery. Costs of the services listed below, among others, vary from $5 to $13, depending on the type of service you select.

| Service | Specifications |
|---|---|
| **Federal Express** | Fed Ex Letter<br>Delivered before next business morning<br>Delivered before next business afternoon<br>Weight limit: 8 ounces |
| **United Parcel Service** | Next Day Air Letter<br>2nd Day Air Letter<br>Weight limit: none, but cost increases with weight |
| **U.S. Postal Service** | Express Mail Next Day Service<br>Weight limit: 8 ounces |

## Leaving Military Service

If you are leaving military service after three or thirty years, you are in for some culture shock. Half the officers and a third of the enlisted men who leave the service are still unemployed after six months. To avoid joining this club, follow these suggestions:

- Don't depend on your military accomplishments to earn you a job. You are starting over in a new ball game. Let *Career Starter* teach you the new rules.

- Use the career office in the college or university where you received your degree or near where you live to provide information and leads.

- Many national search firms have specialists working with former military officers. A few firms specialize in this area.

- You must have a civilian resumé to translate your military accomplishments into corporate terminology (see "Suggested Reading," below).

### *Suggested Reading*

- *Marketing Yourself for a Second Career*
  Col. Doug Carter, The Retired Officers Association, Alexandria, VA, (703) 838-8117

- *Leaving the Military:*
  *Your Guide to Separation and Retirement*
  USAA Foundation, San Antonio, TX, (800) 531-8722

# JOB INTELLIGENCE GATHERING

*First Job: Sinéad O'Connor, singer and songwriter, was a Kiss-o-gram girl who sang birthday greetings while wearing a French maid's outfit.*

*First Job: Lynn Martin, U.S. Representative from Illinois, was a high school English, government and economics teacher.*

**S**ometimes uncommon methods provide a competitive advantage when competing for a job. Try these ideas if you are willing to attempt a different approach:

1. Ask friends to search employee bulletin boards where they work for internal job listings.

2. Call the business reporter of your local newspaper and ask him or her which companies in your chosen field are growing and hiring.

3. Call a commercial loan officer with your local bank. Ask him or her which of the bank's customer companies are growing. Get referrals to key people as well as to other loan officers, accountants and lawyers.

4. Visit nearby restaurants during lunch to meet employees who can tell you which divisions of their companies are growing and need people.

# IMPROVING YOUR PROSPECTS IN A SLUGGISH JOB MARKET

**T**ry these approaches for dealing with a slow-growth job market.

## *Offer to Work for Minimum Wage.*

If you like a company or want to enter a particular field, offer to work for minimum wage. Make sure the job provides the experience you need. Once you are in the company, you will make friends who can help you move to a better job when it becomes available. And, you will have an insider's advantage.

### Free-Lance as a Part-Timer.

Working part-time offers experience with flexibility. It helps build personal networks and may even lead to a full-time job. You can use temporary services or look for work on your own. Temp firms offer more opportunities, but for lower pay. Working part-time on your own means you have to find your own work, but the hourly rates are usually higher.

### Continue Your Education.

Combine academic study with a paid job. Co-op education is a good transition from school to work. If you need a new major or graduate degree for marketability, a co-op is an ideal solution. You get both education and experience. Check with any college or university regarding co-op opportunities.

### Try Internships.

Normally, internships are ideal for students. However, as a graduate, you may be better qualified for the slot. The contacts and experience you gain are extremely valuable, even if the internship is unpaid. Trade and professional organizations are a good source of internship leads.

### Turn Entrepreneur.

If you believe job prospects are bleak and you have a good idea, why not go into business for yourself? Turn a hobby or summer job experience into a money-making venture. It takes little capital to start a service business. You might be able to borrow from your family to start a venture like catering, desktop publishing or home remodeling. And, while prospecting for customers, you will probably get actual job leads. Then you may have some interesting decisions to make regarding working for someone else versus working for yourself.

# How to Use Your Job Prospect Profile

**F**or each person you call or write, start a Job Prospect File. Use this form to record all pertinent information about the jobs you're applying for. Make multiple copies of this form and use a separate form for

## Job Prospect Profile

**Company Name** _____

**Primary Contact** _____ **Title** _____

**Telephone** _____ **Secretary** _____

**Address** _____

_____

_____

**Job Title** _____

**Job Responsibilities** _____

_____

**Job Qualifications** _____

_____

_____

**Company Mission** _____

_____

**Products/Services** _____

_____

**Other Key Contacts** _____

_____

**Referred By** _____

**Resumé Sent To** _____ **Date** _____

**Follow-Up Call** _____ **Date** _____

**Interview (1) with** _____ **Date** _____

**Thank-You Note Sent** _____ **Date** _____

**Interview (2) with** _____ **Date** _____

**Thank-You Note Sent** _____ **Date** _____

**Interview (3) with** _____ **Date** _____

**Thank-You Note Sent** _____ **Date** _____

**Job Offer** _____ **Date** _____

each position. File them alphabetically (by the first initial of each primary contact's last name) after the appropriate Action Log sheet (see page 73). Or, file them in individual folders labeled with the name of the primary contact and company name.

### References

If you can, find out where the company banks, what firm does its accounting, who represents it legally and who its customers are, and then check out the company. Record your feedback here. (For more on this, see the discussion of corporate culture on page 111.)

**Commercial Bank** _____

**Accounting Firm** _____

**Law Firm** _____

**Customers** _____

_____

### Materials Obtained
- ❏ **Annual Report**
- ❏ **Newsletter**
- ❏ **Brochures**
- ❏ **Magazine Articles**
- ❏ **Newspaper Stories**
- ❏ **Organization Chart**
- ❏ **Telephone Directory**
- ❏ **Press Kit**

### Your Own Thoughts

### Attach Business Card Here

PART

SEVEN

# INTERVIEWING

# FOR

# FIRST PLACE

# You Can Master the Situation

The objective of the interview is to convince the interviewer that you are the most qualified potential team member. First place gets the job. Second place provides experience that builds character. Here are some guidelines and tactics you can use to win:

## *Pre-Interview Preparation*

- When scheduling an appointment for an interview, you should ask to receive information about the job and the company if you have not already done so. Better yet, go pick it up yourself, get a good look at the place and meet the secretary. Ask for annual reports, brochures, a press kit (which includes company history, key personnel, biographies, and product/service information), and especially the job description. This will help you prepare and separate you from the competitors.

- Ask for directions and how long it will take to get there. Allow ample time for travel. Arrive twenty minutes early. Don't be sabotaged by unexpected traffic. Wait fifteen minutes outside and review your notes, then walk up to the receptionist five minutes early.

- Read the information and prepare a 30- to 40-word statement (your "infomercial") covering who you are, what your job goal is, and two or three reasons why your skills fit the job requirements. For example: *"I've just graduated from Virginia Commonwealth University with a BA in English. My goal is to work as a staff writer with a company like yours. My interest and experience in proposal and report writing for the EPA matches your company's environmental business."*

*In 1992, the average salary offer to students receiving doctoral degrees in psychology was $38,452, while the average offer to students receiving bachelor's degrees in chemical engineering was $39,203.*

**Arsenio Hall, comedian, actor and talk show host, earned a bachelor's degree in general speech from Kent State University.**

**Jay Leno, comedian and talk show host, earned his bachelor's degree in speech therapy at Emerson College in Boston.**

- Practice saying your self-description aloud. Use a tape recorder and listen to how you sound. Are you enthusiastic? Too serious? Does your voice shake?

- Think about how the interview might go. Prepare your questions and your responses to the hard questions you anticipate. Repeat this process until you are confident and as prepared as you can be.

- Videotape practice interviews with friends who have had successful interviews and can offer tips. If a VCR is not available, practice in front of a mirror.

- Never turn down an interview. Interviewing is a skill that you can improve, but practice interviewing is no substitute for the real thing. In addition, an interview can produce referrals.

### Arriving For the Interview

- Normally you will have to wait a few minutes before your interviewer meets you. Be friendly to the receptionist. The interviewer may ask for his or her impression of you. If it is policy to fill out an application, do so even if you already have a resumé. Most firms are required to obtain a standard job application from every applicant.

- While you are waiting for the interviewer, peruse one of the magazines that are on the coffee table, or read the newspaper. Don't pull out a novel from your briefcase (unless you're interviewing with a publisher or other creative organization—the book might prompt an interesting discussion that you and the interviewer might benefit from). It's fine to read a book at an airport, but in an interview setting, it often is out of place. It's better to show interest in business, current events or the industry.

- When the interviewer comes to greet you, smile broadly, offer a firm handshake and address him or her formally—Mr. Smith, Ms. Jones or Mrs. Green. Practice handshaking with your friends and avoid a limp handshake. A simple thing like a weak handshake can get the interview off to a poor start.

- If you're interviewing with a woman, ask the receptionist beforehand what title (Miss, Ms. or Mrs.) the interviewer prefers.

## Interviewing to Win

- The objective of the interview is to convince the interviewer that you are the most qualified potential team member.

- Do your homework beforehand. Reading a company's annual report, brochures, newsletters and job description can make you an informed candidate.

- Almost always, the interviewer will begin by saying, "Tell me about yourself." It is best to answer this question *after* the job has been described to you so that you can tailor your response accordingly. If you have to talk first, present your prepared self-description.

- Put yourself in the interviewer's shoes; listen and try to respond from his or her perspective.

- If the interviewer tries to engage you in a debate, say you're not knowledgeable enough about the subject to discuss it.

- If the interviewer tries to antagonize you, be as charming and polite as possible. Maintain control and wrestle with the issues, not your emotions.

- If your interviewer is shy, distracted or unprepared, you will have to take control of the interview. Talk

*Richard Gephardt, U.S. Representative from Missouri, earned a bachelor's in speech and drama at Northwestern University.*

*First Job:
Danny DeVito,
actor and director,
parked cars for
two years.*

*First Job:
Bruce Willis, actor,
drove work crews
around in a truck
at a DuPont plant.*

about your skills and experience and how they relate to the job you're interviewing for. Ask questions. (See page 107, "Interviewing the Interviewer.")

- If the interviewer raises an area of personal interest such as sports or music, you should talk sports or music if you can. Follow his or her lead, and don't attempt to show you know more than he or she does about the subject.

- Prove you are capable of performing rather than merely describing. Provide examples and illustrations of what you have accomplished. For example, merely stating that you are good at selling won't get you the job. Prove to the interviewer that you can sell by selling the benefits you offer for this job. Talk about your sales successes.

- If you are overqualified for the job, you can state that you are willing to start at the bottom and work your way up. For example, you may be qualified to be a sales representative, but you may have to start as a sales administrator, handling telephone calls and paperwork until a sales representative position is available to you.

- If you do not understand the question, say:
*"I'm sorry, I don't understand the question."* Or, *"Could you please rephrase the question?"*

- Do not fabricate, guess or generalize, and do not engage the interviewer in a debate.

- Do not say why the job would be good or bad for you personally. That is not the point during the interview. The point is to emphasize how you can help the company.

- Do not talk yourself out of the job by rambling. Be brief, be right, then be quiet.

- At the conclusion of the interview, indicate that you would love to work for the company if that is what you think and feel.

## Post-Interview Actions

- Send a note thanking the interviewer for his or her consideration, expressing your interest in the job and reminding the interviewer how well your qualifications fit the position.

- Attach your interview notes to your Job Prospect Profile (see Part Six, pages 90-91) and place them in your *Career Starter* notebook or in a folder with the name of the interviewer and company on the tab.

- Prepare a list of positives and negatives to help you make a decision if you receive an offer (see Part Eight, page 123).

- Call the interviewer if you have not received a response when one is expected.

## Suggested Reading

- *Sweaty Palms: The Neglected Art of Being Interviewed*
  H. Anthony Medley, Ten Speed Press

- *The Perfect Interview*
  John D. Drake, AMACOM

## Sample Interview Thank-You Letter

Virginia C. Union
2323 Sullivan Ballou Avenue
Bull Run, Virginia  22090
(703) 555-1234

July 20, 1993

Ms. Jill Senate
Director of Communications
Washington Associates, Inc.
1801 Pennsylvania Avenue, N.W.
Washington, DC  20000

Dear Ms. Senate:

Thank you for the opportunity to discuss the possibility of joining your organization as a staff writer. Our discussion was helpful in showing how well my English degree, word processing skills and writing experience fit the position.

My specific experience in writing proposals and reports for EPA would be beneficial for your new wetlands project. And, I would enjoy working with your staff on the project.

I appreciate the time you spent with me and look forward to hearing from you. In the meantime, thank you for your consideration.

Sincerely,

Virginia C. Union

## Pointers to Increase Your Comfort

1. **Maintain good posture.**
Sit comfortably, but lean slightly forward to look alert. Smile!

2. **Take a note pad with you.**
Have a few key points and some important questions already written down. The information will be available to you as you take notes.

3. **Use natural gestures.**
They will make you appear enthusiastic.

4. **Pay attention.**
Maintain eye contact, but don't get into a staring contest. Listen attentively.

5. **Be friendly.**
Establish a rapport with the interviewer to make the process easier for both of you.

6. **Be likable.**
Try to relate to your interviewer and to what he or she is saying.

7. **Be courteous.**
Feel free to compliment your interviewer when he or she asks good questions or makes valid points.

8. **Avoid "yes" and "no" answers.**
Strike a balance. Show the interviewer that you know what you're talking about, but don't go on forever.

9. **Do not smoke, chew gum or fidget.**

10. **Avoid getting drawn into a discussion of controversial topics.**
If the discussion could be pertinent to the job, be diplomatic.

11. **Do not criticize anyone or anything.**

12. **Never interrupt the interviewer.**
Don't finish his or her sentences.

## What Companies Want

The ideal employee—at any level—is highly motivated, uses common sense, pays attention to detail, can anticipate and solve problems, and is a team player. The following presents a profile of a desirable employee:

- Shows intelligence and initiative.

- Communicates clearly.

- Sets a good example for others.

- Anticipates and solves problems diplomatically.

- Displays courtesy, charm and character.

- Is self-sufficient yet contributes as a team member.

- Alters plans flexibly when required.

- Handles details while possessing an overall perspective.

- Is oriented toward accomplishment rather than activity.

- Follows instructions.

- Meets deadlines.

- Does the right things right the first time.

*Special Note:* These are all qualities you can assess in yourself even if you've only worked as a student.

## Questions You May Be Asked

- **Tell me about yourself. How would you describe yourself?**

  *Present your "infomercial." You may then add information regarding your early years, extracurricular activities and summer or part-time jobs in response to a specific inquiry.*

- **Who are your heroes?**

  *This is an attempt to get to know you better. Have one person in mind with a story that highlights your interests and strengths.*

- **What are your career goals?**

  *You will know your answers based on your reading of Part One. Now relate your answer to the job opportunity you are discussing.*

- **What do you like doing the most?**

  *Keep your response in line with the situation you are discussing. You may mention an avocation, but don't get trapped into talking about vacationing or socializing.*

- **Describe your most rewarding experience.**

  *Keep your response oriented to the current situation.*

- **How did you like living in (home town)?**

  *Describe the benefits of living in a small or large community.*

- **Why did you attend (name) college?**

  *State your reasons, such as size, available major, cost, for your decision.*

- **Why did you major in (name)?**

  *Relate your major to your interests and skills.*

- **How much of your college education did you pay for yourself?**

  *This is an opportunity to score big time by giving a percentage figure and then listing scholarships, co-ops, part-time jobs, internships, and summer jobs related to the job for which you are interviewing and that provided the funds for your education. If your parents paid for everything, emphasize what you have done on your own—volunteer work or community service.*

- **How did you get involved in (extracurricular activity)?**

  *Tell how you became interested in the activity, then attempt to link it to one of the job requirements or desired personal traits.*

## Questions You May Be Asked (cont'd.)

- **Describe the ideal job for you.**

  *Describe the job situation you are discussing in your own words. Don't parrot the exact job description or you will be perceived as uninspired or uninterested.*

- **What are your greatest strengths or weaknesses?**

  *Match one or two strengths to the job requirement. Regarding weaknesses, be honest but turn a negative into a positive. For example, you might say, "In school I tended to procrastinate at times. But, you know, I enjoyed working under the resulting pressure. And I always meet deadlines."*

- **How did you learn of our company?**

  *State the referral, job listing or advertisement or your own research that resulted in the interview.*

- **What do you know about the company?**

  *Based on your preparation, you'll know about its products/services, history, reputation, large customers, growth and profitability.*

- **Why do you want to work for us?**

  *Describe how you can make a contribution to meeting company goals.*

- **What appeals to you about the job?**

  *Describe two or three factors that are attractive to you.*

- **Tell me about your previous job experience.**

  *Be specific in terms of your accomplishments in summer, part-time or full-time jobs. Include volunteer or club experience and any other activity that relates to the situation you are discussing.*

- **Why should we hire you?**

  *Match the benefits from your education, skills and experience to the job requirements.*

- **How do you handle pressure?**

  *Tell the interviewer you enjoy working under pressure.*

- **What about working evenings and weekends?**

  *If you can do so honestly, tell the interviewer that you believe in doing what it takes to get the job done efficiently and in a timely fashion.*

  *If you have real limits on your time, say so, and live with the consequences. Be honest with yourself and your employer. If you don't want to work 70 hours a week, don't take a job that you think will require that much overtime.*

- **Are you able to travel? Can you relocate?**

  *Be honest.*

- **What are your salary requirements?**

  *Answer with a question, "What is the salary range for this position?" If no range exists, implement what you will have learned on page 113.*

- **What other jobs are you considering?**

  *Keep your answer related to this field or type of job, and don't be too specific.*

- **May I have a list of references?**

  *Provide references related to your work experience. One academic reference is adequate.*

- **Is there anything more you would like to know?**

  *Use this as an opportunity to clarify any issues or to make any points you wish to make that may not have been discussed. Be curious, and show your interest.*

# QUESTIONS THAT SHOULDN'T BE ASKED

*John Hughes, filmmaker, writer and producer, dropped out of the University of Alabama during his junior year.*

*Barry Levinson, filmmaker, writer and producer, dropped out of the broadcast journalism program at American University after seven years of stop-and-go.*

In many situations, it is against the law for any employer to invade your privacy. But many times employers *do* ask illegal questions, directly or indirectly. Those include:

- How old are you?

- How is your health?

- What is your marital status?

- What is your religion?

- Do you plan to have children?

- What happens if your spouse gets transferred?

You may also encounter questions or comments that seem inappropriate or make you feel uneasy. For example, an interviewer might compliment you or remark upon your appearance to a degree you're uncomfortable with.

It is important to note that certain employers, like churches, can ask your religious affiliation because the position may entail promoting a particular religion. However, unlawful questions are sometimes asked accidentally.

Assuming that the question is improper, what should you do? Probably the worst thing to do would be to respond angrily that the interviewer's question is illegal. The rapport you may have shared with the interviewer until that moment will be undoubtedly shattered. On the other hand, pay attention to such caution lights. Do you really want to work for a person or company that raises these questions? Regardless, maintain a polite manner. You don't want to burn any bridges. You can do any of the following:

- Answer the question tactfully if you want to.

- Say: *"Why do you ask?"*

- Try returning to a discussion of qualifications by asking: *"Could you tell me how this is related to job performance?"*

- Try humor. If asked about age, you could say: *"Put it this way. I haven't been carded lately!"* Or, about religion: *"I belong to the church of hard work!"*

- Say politely: *"I'm not clear on how this is pertinent to the job function."*

Many women in their twenties and thirties are often asked in interviews whether they are planning to have children soon. If asked this question, you may say, "no." You can always change your mind. And, there are always unplanned pregnancies. When one young woman was asked this question, she responded that children weren't in her plans for a couple of years and that when and if she had children, she intended to get full-time help. That comment immediately satisfied the interviewer, and she got the job.

You should never lie. However, when people illegally pry into your personal life, you do not owe it to them to disqualify yourself. You can always be vague without lying. Never feel obligated to say something you don't want to say.

## *What If I Have a Disability?*

The Americans With Disabilities Act (ADA) states that an employer with 25 or more employees cannot discriminate against a qualified prospective employee with a known disability. The ADA also states that upon hiring the disabled individual, the employer must provide reasonable accommodation, unless undue hardship would result.

This means that if your disability is obvious, interview questions must be posed in terms of your ability to perform essential job functions. In addition, no questions can be asked about prior claims for worker's compensation. Finally, no pre-offer medical exam can be required, and a post-offer exam can be required only if it is required for all employees.

However, you should be aware of two issues. First, you have the responsibility to inform any employer of your disability. Second, an employer can require documentation of your disability.

The key issue during an interview is to keep the focus on your ability to perform essential job functions. It is critical to match your skills with the requirements stated in the job description. As always, straightforwardness and humor are the best approaches. The reality is, regardless of what the law says, you will still have to convince your potential employer that you can do the job. Chances are you can do it better than many people.

# INTERVIEWING THE INTERVIEWER

**R**emember, ours is a society of choices. You have a choice of employer. You are looking for a good fit—or chemistry—with the interviewer and a compatibility with the company's culture.

The interviewer represents the company. Would you like to work with this person? Why? Why not? You also need to assess:

- Is the interviewer a real person or is he or she playing the "boss" role? Is he or she representing the company well?

- Is the company's management style formal or informal? Hands-on or distant? People, numbers or technically oriented?

First impressions count. It is okay to be skeptical. Sometimes the most dumb-sounding questions are the most profound. So don't worry about looking foolish. If you have a question, ask it in a positive way.

Also, listen carefully, observe closely and remember the acronym **GIVE**, described in the accompanying box:

## The Meaning of GIVE

- *Goals*
  Are the company's and your personal goals aligned? How does the company treat its employees? Does it offer continuing education programs?
- *Integrity*
  Can you trust these people? Are they open or secretive? Do they deal in half-truths?
- *Values*
  Is the company's beliefs compatible with yours? Does it protect the environment? Does it promote from within?
- *Ethics*
  Will your employer encourage you to break the rules? Is the interviewer asking questions he or she should not be asking? Is there high employee turnover? Why?

## Twenty Good Questions to Ask the Interviewer

You will be judged by your questions as well as by your answers. Here are twenty good questions to ask:

1. May I take notes?

2. How did you get started in the company? What made you successful?

3. How would you describe the company's business focus/mission?

4. What are the trends in sales and profits?

5. Who are the company's major competitors, and what are the company's competitive strengths?

6. Where is the company going in the next three to five years?

7. How would you describe the corporate culture?

8. What are the specific responsibilities of the job?

9. What type of person are you looking for?

10. What qualities would the ideal candidate have?

11. What would you expect of me in this position, and what could I expect in the future?

12. Is this a new position or has the job been held by someone else? If the latter is so, is the person still with the company?

13. What about others who started in this position over the past few years? Have any of them been promoted? Into what positions?

**14.** Where can this job lead for a top performer?

**15.** What resources are available to perform this job?

**16.** How will I be evaluated? By whom? When?

**17.** What education and training programs does the company provide?

**18.** How will the final hiring decision be made? By whom? When?

**19.** Is there anything else I need to know?

**20.** If you want the job, say: *"I am very interested in this position. What is the next step?"*

Close by thanking the interviewer for the opportunity to discuss the situation.

## Five Deadly Questions

The following questions will kill your chances of getting the job:

### 1. What is my salary?

Do not ask about salary unless the interviewer raises the subject first. This may not happen until the second interview or even later, when an offer is extended. As curious as you may be, you must be patient or risk leaving the impression that you are more interested in money than in being a team player.

### 2. How much vacation and sick leave will I get?

Asking about these makes you seem as though you are asking for time off before you have even started the job. Some interviewers may perceive this as a sign of lack of dedication, however unfairly. Naturally, you want to get this information. However, the best way to do it is by asking for a copy of the personnel manual, by talking to the personnel administrator, or by speaking with other employees before taking the job. You should be briefed on benefits at the appropriate time. If not, just ask, "What about the benefits?" after the salary issue has been raised.

### 3. How big is my office?

A dedicated team player produces good work regardless of the office environment. Questions regarding office size may be seen as a concern about job appearance rather than the essential elements of the job. Usually, during a tour of the operation, you will be shown the area where you will work.

### 4. When will I be promoted?

This question is impossible to answer. Promotion depends on timing and your performance. Opportunities for promotion depend on change, such as growth and turnover. Your suitability for promotion depends on your prior performance together with your abilities to plan, organize and get others to perform. Questions regarding promotion should focus on opportunities for advancement, rather than on a commitment that cannot be given.

### 5. Any negative question!

Any question that is negative or solicits a negative response places the interviewer in an unfavorable and sometimes awkward position. In addition, it makes you look like a negative person. Ask all questions in a positive manner.

# WHAT ABOUT CORPORATE CULTURE?

To many of us, corporate culture is a vague term. What does it mean? And, why is it relevant to your job search?

Corporate culture is the set of beliefs, traits and processes that a company practices over time. Some companies are caring, others are challenging. Some focus on customer service while others value product quality first. In most cases, management has created and nurtured the culture in its own image. In other cases, corporate culture is just propaganda.

For your job search, the corporate culture issue is twofold. First, is it real? Does the company practice what it preaches? And two, do you want to join the club? Can you embrace the culture as your own?

To analyze any corporate culture, listen for key claims and slogans, such as:

- Customer Service

- Empowerment

- Total Quality Management

- Excellence

You can get a good sense of a company's corporate culture by paying attention to the office environment and what goes on around you while you are interviewing at the company. Look and listen for hints in the elevator, cafeteria and parking lot. Ask yourself the following questions:

- How are you treated by the receptionist?

- Is the office clean, neat and organized?

*In 1992, undergrads in computer programming were offered salaries that were, on average, 14% higher than the year before. Criminal justice majors were offered 10.9% less.*

- How do people dress?

- Are the employees busy?

- Are employees gossiping about one another?

- Is there a spirit of teamwork?

- Are the company's executives accessible to all employees?

- Is the atmosphere formal or informal?

During the interview, ask questions like:

- How are decisions made?

- How are employees rewarded for a job well done?

- Does the company promote from within?

- How do you learn about company news?

- How is work delegated?

- Who has authority to sign for what?

Independent sources are always worthwhile when checking out a company's corporate culture. Trade associations, chambers of commerce, local business reporters, bankers, public accountants and lawyers can be very helpful. In addition, customers, suppliers and former employees can provide valuable insight into the real culture of an organization. Ask about the company's reputation as an employer. Compare your findings from external sources with what you were told by the interviewer.

In the final analysis, the key issues are: Can you function effectively within this culture? Can you perform as a member of this team? Do you fit in?

## SALARY NEGOTIATIONS

**M**ost companies have a salary range for each job. Your ability to negotiate within that range depends on your qualifications together with the salary information you have learned from doing your homework. There is no substitute for knowing the facts and using them for your benefit. Here are some effective ways to deal with the salary issues.

What do you do when the interviewer asks difficult questions like these:

- Have you thought about salary?

- What are your salary requirements?

- What is the minimum salary you will accept?

The best approach, if possible, is to reverse the issue by answering the question with a question. Your response might be:

- *"What is the salary range for this position?"*

- *"Most of my peers who are also graduating business majors have been receiving offers in the $20,000 to $24,000 range. What range is authorized for this position?"*

Be prepared:

- Have a salary figure in mind based on the pricing issues discussed in Part Five, "When You're Marketing Yourself."

- When completing an application, under "salary required" always write in "negotiable" or "competitive."

*Douglas Wilder, governor of Virginia, earned a bachelor's in chemistry from Virginia Union University in Richmond.*

*General Colin Powell, Chairman of the Joint Chiefs of Staff, earned a bachelor's degree in geology at the City College of New York.*

When you're ready to negotiate:

- Equate your salary requirement to something sub-stantive, such as a survey, other offers you have received or an explanation of why you require what you're asking.

- Focus on the smallest difference between your figure and the offer—$20,000 versus $22,000 is about 96 cents an hour. Present the 96 cents difference rather than the $2,000 difference, then go for the maxi-mum amount.

- Be prepared to split the difference fifty-fifty as the final resolution.

# INTERVIEW DRESS FOR MEN

People make judgments within the first five minutes of an interview. If you appear well-groomed and polished, you will make a good first impression.

A solid or pin-striped gray or navy suit is always a good investment. However, if your budget doesn't allow you to buy a suit, wear a navy blazer and gray trousers. In general, dress above what the job requires. Consider colors you look good in. Avoid herringbone or tiny plaids, which tend to "dance" in the eyes of some people.

Remember to wear a cotton undershirt with your shirt, even in hot weather (it makes the shirt look whiter). Take your shirts to a commercial laundry or dry cleaner and ask for starch (they come out looking much better than you could do at home). Put on a fresh shirt from the cleaners just before the interview. Check your shirt to see whether it needs pressing, and keep your shoes freshly shined. Also:

- Wear long socks so no skin will show when you cross your legs.

- If you wear suspenders, don't also wear a belt. The suspenders should match or complement your tie. It will be easier to coordinate suspenders and ties if the suspenders are solid or striped (burgundy/navy or red/navy).

- The tie should be silk and either striped, paisley or have a small pattern, such as dots. Avoid large, elaborate patterns or ties with too many colors.

- Get a haircut or wear a style appropriate to the work situation you're interested in. For example, a ponytail that might be appropriate at some advertising agencies or radio stations might not be appropriate in a law office.

*First Jobs: Warren Beatty, actor and filmmaker, was a dishwasher, bricklayer's assistant and cocktail lounge pianist.*

- Leave your earring at home, unless you're confident about the work situation.

- Don't wear the exact same outfit twice to the same company. At least change your tie. Make note of what you wear to each interview on your Action Log or Job Prospect Profile.

# INTERVIEW DRESS FOR WOMEN

Remember that one's dress and grooming send out powerful messages to a prospective employer. If you want to be absolutely appropriate in most corporate settings, choose a classic suit in navy, gray or black (or a lighter neutral in summer or warmer climates). A conservative dress with a jacket would also work provided it is not too low cut, girlish or bright. Although a suit or dress is preferable, a navy blazer and classic gray skirt (wool in winter, linen in summer) can be worn. Make sure you choose a suit with a classic cut that fits well. If necessary, take the suit to a tailor for alterations. On no occasion should you wear pants. As for the blouse, keep it simple, subdued and jewel-necked in a natural-looking fabric.

- Shorter skirts are acceptable, provided that the skirt meets the top of the knee. Do not interview in a short skirt unless you are looking for a position with a company that makes or sells short skirts.

- Clinging clothes, flashy or glittery fingernails, open-toe shoes and dangling earrings are all inappropriate for an interview. Get a good haircut, and if your hair tends to look a little wild, wear it up, back or with a headband. If you wear nail polish, make sure none of the polish is chipped and that the color is either clear or pale pink.

- Wear just a few pieces of jewelry. Stud earrings, watch, pearls and one gold chain are sufficient. Don't wear more than one ring on each hand. Pearl studs and a strand of pearls can add a classic touch.

- Pantyhose, even in the summer, are a must. Bare legs might escape the attention of a male interviewer, but the odds are that any woman who interviews you would notice. It's a good idea to carry a spare pair in your briefcase or purse.

- Briefcases are optional, but find one proportional to your size or you'll look like you're carrying your Dad's. What you should avoid, however, is carrying a tote or shopping bag to the interview. If you need to wear athletic shoes en route to the interview, carry a briefcase large enough to conceal them. Change into your pumps outside the building. You will be less nervous doing this away from the gaze of the company receptionist, and you can concentrate on observing the company employees and the office atmosphere.

- Don't wear the exact same outfit twice to the same company. At least wear a different blouse or other accessories. Make note of what you wear to each interview on your Action Log or Job Prospect Profile.

Remember, how you apply this advice will depend on the place of employment, type of business and part of the country, including the city. A woman applying for a graphic design, architecture, ad agency, retail or other creative position may have more leeway with the way she dresses and may need to use it.

*Overall in 1991, women earned 70 cents for every dollar earned by men.*

## OBTAINING VALUE
## FROM EACH INTERVIEW

*Faye Wattleton, president of the Planned Parenthood Federation of America, earned a bachelor's in nursing from Ohio State University and a master's in maternal and infant health care from Columbia University, with a specialty in midwifery.*

Rejection letters are inevitable. Do not take them personally. Most of the time, there was a better candidate for the job. However, you can use the situation to obtain suggestions for improvement and referrals.

Obtain some real value from each rejection letter. Don't let a simple "no" affect you in a negative way. Call each person who has sent a rejection letter and thank him or her for considering you. Ask for suggestions for improving your resumé, interview skills or job search direction. Write the suggestions on the Job Search Improvement Suggestions form on the next page.

Remember to ask for referrals to other organizations or people who might be able to use your abilities or capabilities. Try to obtain two or three leads.

Finally, ask what the person would do if he or she were in your situation. Who would he or she call? Above all, never, never, never give up. Keep calling. Keep learning. Keep improving. You will be successful.

## Job Campaign Improvement Suggestions

### How to Use Your Improvement Work Sheet

The farther you progress in your job campaign, the more you will discover what works and what doesn't. Take the time to evaluate your job search techniques and use this work sheet to jot down how you can strengthen your strategy. Keep multiple copies in your *Career Starter* notebook and consider filling it out weekly and/or after each job interview.

### Modify Strategy or Tactics

_____

_____

_____

### Revise Resumé

_____

_____

_____

### Acquire New Skills

_____

_____

_____

### Improve Interview Techniques

_____

_____

_____

### Obtain More Referrals

_____

_____

_____

### My Own Thoughts

_____

_____

_____

# TIME
# TO MAKE
# A DECISION

# GO OR NO-GO?

Once you receive an offer, you normally have a short period of time, such as two to three weeks, to respond. In most situations, multiple offers are not received simultaneously. Therefore, each offer must be considered on its own merits.

Your decision is a judgment call. The key is to make the call based on the elements that are important to you: compatibility with your long-term and short-term goals, competency in performing daily tasks, ability to work with your supervisor for mutually beneficial results and comfort with the corporate culture.

If you have serious doubts about an offer, it is best to meet with whomever is making the offer to resolve your doubts. If you can't resolve them, do not accept the offer. Don't fool yourself and waste months or years of your life. On the other hand, don't reject an offer based on trivial concerns, such as not having your own parking space or having to share an office.

Keep compensation and benefits in the proper perspective. Sometimes non-monetary rewards, such as paid educational benefits, are more important than starting salary in the long run. And, there are times when a lower starting salary will be outweighed by near-term promotion opportunities.

Once you have decided for or against a job offer, it is appropriate to extend a written acceptance or refusal to the company that made you the offer. Your letter can be short and to the point, and should always be courteous (see the sample letters on pages 124 and 125).

*Bill Cosby, comedian, actor and author, dropped out of the physical education program at Temple University in Philadelphia during his sophomore year. In 1977, he earned his doctoral degree in education from the University of Massachusetts.*

# JOB OFFER EVALUATION

**S**coring an offer will help you analyze the situation. It will not make the decision for you. However, it will provide a structured and consistent approach to thinking about an offer. And, you may modify the list to suit your personal perspective. Also, you may want to review Part One, "Why Will You Work?", regarding career suitability and quality-of-life issues. It, too, will provide a framework for considering an offer.

Make one copy of the form for each prospective employer who extends an offer. File it after the appropriate Job Prospect Profile Work Sheet.

On your Evaluation Form, score each item from one (lowest) to ten (highest). The maximum score is 180. Because the scoring is subjective, you can set your own range for consideration. For example, 140 might be the appropriate cut-off for a generous scorer, while 100 might be more reasonable for a critical scorer. Remember, the score does not make the decision, you do.

# Evaluation Form

**Company Name** _____
**Primary Contact** _____

### The Position                                                          *Score*
- How does the position fit with my career goals?                    _____
- Will I have meaningful responsibilities that can be measured?       _____
- Will I be visible to key people in the company?                     _____
- Do I really want this job?                                          _____

### Your Supervisor
- Can I work with this person?                                        _____
- Do I respect this person's values?                                  _____
- Is this person liked and respected by his or her co-workers
  and supervisors?                                                    _____

### The Company
- Is the company growing?                                             _____
- Is the company profitable?                                          _____
- How does the company rank compared with its competitors?            _____
- Is there opportunity for advancement?                               _____
- Do I fit in?                                                        _____

### Compensation
- Can I live on the salary? If not, can I supplement it with income
  elsewhere and make it a livable salary?                             _____
- Are the benefits adequate?                                          _____
- Are training and educational programs available?                   _____

### Related Factors
- How easy is commuting?                                              _____
- How affordable is housing?                                          _____
- How compatible is the location with my lifestyle?                   _____

                                                          *Total*      _____

### My Own Thoughts

# RESPONSE TO OFFERS

**O**nce you have decided for or against a job offer, it's appropriate to extend a written acceptance or refusal to the company that made you the offer. Your letter can be short and to the point. The following letters are examples of how to courteously accept or refuse a job offer.

## Sample Acceptance Letter

**Virginia C. Union**
**2323 Sullivan Ballou Avenue**
**Bull Run, Virginia 22090**
**(703) 555-1234**

August 16, 1993

Ms. Jill Senate
Director of Communications
Washington Associates, Inc.
1801 Pennsylvania Avenue, N.W.
Washington, DC 20000

Dear Ms. Senate:

I am pleased to accept your offer to join Washington Associates, Inc., as a staff writer at an annual salary of $20,000. I am confident that my responsibilities will be both interesting and challenging.

I look forward to my new career with Washington Associates and will report to your office at 8:30 A.M. on September 7, 1993, as agreed. Thank you.

Sincerely,

Virginia C. Union

## Sample Rejection Letter

**Virginia C. Union**
**2323 Sullivan Ballou Avenue**
**Bull Run, Virginia  22090**
**(703) 555-1234**

August 16, 1993

Ms. Jill Senate
Director of Communications
Washington Associates, Inc.
1801 Pennsylvania Avenue, N.W.
Washington, DC  20000

Dear Ms. Senate:

Thank you for your offer to join Washington Associates, Inc., as a staff writer. Unfortunately, I am unable to accept the offer because I have accepted a similar position with another company.

I appreciate the opportunity to be considered for employment with Washington Associates, Inc.  Best wishes for your continued success.

Sincerely,


Virginia C. Union

# TWENTY TIPS FOR SUCCESS

*Gary Larson, creator of "The Far Side," earned a bachelor's in communications from Washington State University, while also taking courses in zoology, ornithology, entomology, archeology and anthropology.*

**C**ongratulations, you've accepted the job you wanted. You have been hired as a contributing team member. Put the team first, "me" second. As a team member, you will be expected to produce. Anticipate, don't wait for detailed directions. Get ahead of the pack. Beat deadlines. Exceed expectations. Then ask yourself, "How can I do better?"

Beware of office politics. Learn to work within the system and without being manipulated. Deal with the facts—who, what, when, where, how, why—together with your recommendations for solving problem situations. Finally, observe the following proven rules for succeeding at work.

1. **Be visible.** Introduce yourself to everyone. Relate well to others.

2. **Assume responsibility for your own success.** Don't make excuses.

3. **Accept new risks as opportunities to expand your potential.** Don't be afraid to make a mistake—just don't make the same one twice.

4. **Be willing to pay your dues.** Volunteer for tasks no one else wants to do with pleasantness and good humor.

5. **Make your supervisor's decision to hire you a good decision.** Hopefully, he or she will become a mentor who can help guide your career development. Always keep your supervisor informed.

6. **Be a productive, pleasant and effective team player.** Try to suggest creative solutions to tough problems.

7. **Learn to observe with a "third eye and ear."** People

don't always say what they mean. Observe actions as well as words.

8. **Don't go to meetings unprepared.** Always take notes and highlight those points you want your supervisor to know. Maintain a meetings diary.

9. **Focus on performing your job as best you can.** Don't worry about how others are performing.

10. **Avoid other peoples' problems and miseries.** Don't take sides in personal battles. Deal with the issues, not the personalities.

11. **Get to work early and leave late.** It is amazing how much you can accomplish without people and telephone interruptions.

12. **Respect other people's values.** Different does not mean inferior. Respect is the foundation for successful relationships.

13. **Learn to separate facts from opinions, issues from feelings.** Focus on defining the problem, then solving it diplomatically.

14. **Negotiate differences of opinion.** Team success depends on mutual agreement. Don't get into "we" versus "they" arguments. Attacking, condemning and fighting leads to team failure.

15. **Take advantage of every educational and training opportunity.** Improve your abilities and learn new skills. Go for consistent personal growth, not instant perfection.

16. **Try to do the right things right the first time.** Then improve your efforts next time—and every time.

17. **Honor your commitments.** Make sure you deliver

*Spike Lee, filmmaker and actor, earned his bachelor's in mass communications at Morehouse College in Atlanta.*

*First Job: Madonna, singer and actress, was a figure model for artists.*

*First Job: John Mellencamp, musician, singer and songwriter, was a telephone installer.*

what you agreed to deliver when you agreed to deliver it—no excuses.

18. **Always set the example.** If you can remember this one rule, everything else will fall into place.

19. **Learn to deal with day-to-day frustrations.** Humor, optimism and confidence help. Build confidence through many small victories.

20. **Have a life away from the office.** Enjoy an avocation to break the work routine. If you play as hard as you work and work as hard as you play, both parts of your life will be fun.

## Suggested Reading

• *Kiplinger's Take Charge of Your Career*
  Daniel Moreau, Kiplinger Books

# ONE FOR THE ROAD

**N**ow that you've made it through the process of starting or restarting your career, it's time to close the book—but not to throw it away. Be sure to save this volume and the personal *Career Starter* notebook that you've created. Keep these resources on hand for that inevitable moment when it's time again to assess your needs, desires and situation and engage in planning, organizing and conducting a job campaign. You'll also have fun looking at this record and realizing how far you have come in your personal and career development.

Remember, too, that your newly developed network of friends, family and acquaintances have real value—now and in the future. They can continue to provide support to you and your endeavors. Just be sure to keep in touch and to reciprocate. And never forgetting how you were helped, volunteer to help others who need your assistance.

Finally, best wishes for many successful careers ahead.